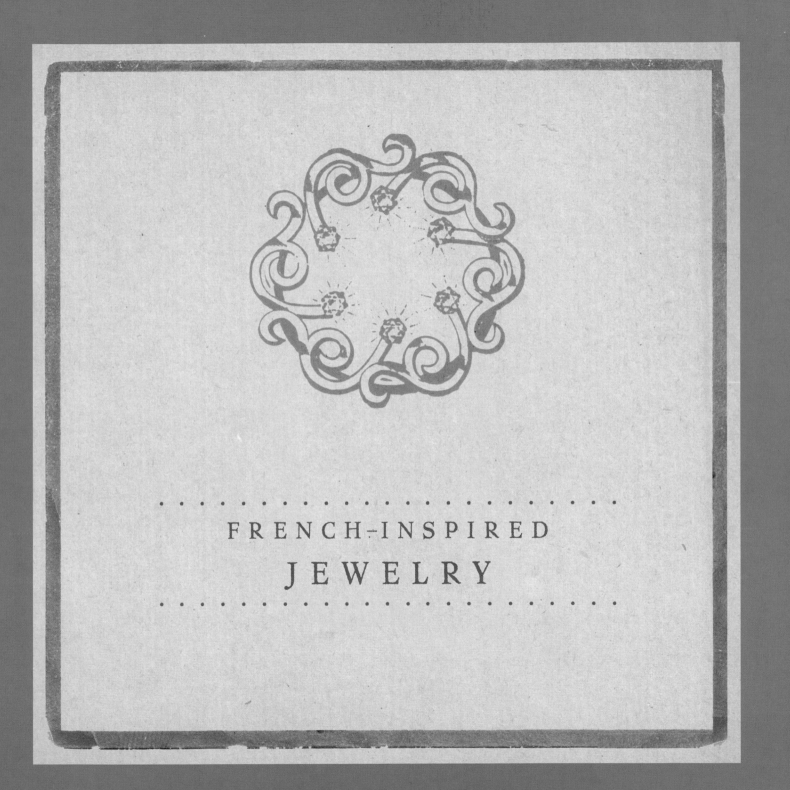

FRENCH-INSPIRED
JEWELRY

FRENCH-INSPIRED
JEWELRY

Creating with vintage beads, buttons & baubles

Kaari Meng

LARK BOOKS
A Division of Sterling Publishing Co., Inc.
New York / London

A Red Lips 4 Courage Communications, Inc. book
www.redlips4courage.com
Eileen Cannon Paulin, *President*
Catherine Risling, *Director of Editorial*
Editor: Catherine Risling
Copy Editor: Lisa Anderson
Book Designer: Jon Zabala
Photographer: Zachary Williams
Photo Stylist: Kaari Meng
Illustrations: Janet Takahashi

Library of Congress Cataloging-in-Publication Data

Meng, Kaari.
French-inspired jewelry: creating with vintage beads,
buttons & baubles /
Kaari Meng.
        p. cm.
Includes index.
ISBN-13: 978-1-60059-096-2 (hc-plc with jacket : alk. paper)
ISBN-10: 1-60059-096-9 (hc-plc with jacket : alk. paper)
1. Beadwork. 2. Jewelry making. 3. Decoration and
ornament--France--Themes, motives. I. Title.
TT860.M48 2007
745.58'2--dc22

10 9 8 7 6 5 4 3

Published by Lark Books,
A Division of Sterling Publishing Co., Inc.
387 Park Avenue South, New York, NY 10016

Text © 2007, Kaari Meng
Photography © 2007, Red Lips 4 Courage Communications, Inc.
Illustrations © 2007, Red Lips 4 Courage Communications, Inc.

Distributed in Canada by Sterling Publishing,
c/o Canadian Manda Group, 165 Dufferin St.
Toronto, Ontario, Canada M6K 3H6

Distributed in the United Kingdom by
GMC Distribution Services,
Castle Place, 166 High Street, Lewes,
East Sussex, England BN7 1XU

Distributed in Australia by Capricorn Link
(Australia) Pty Ltd.,
P.O. Box 704, Windsor, NSW 2756 Australia

The written instructions, photographs, designs, patterns, and projects in this volume are intended for the personal use of the reader and may be reproduced for that purpose only. Any other use, especially commercial use, is forbidden under law without written permission of the copyright holder.

Every effort has been made to ensure that all the information in this book is accurate. However, due to differing conditions, tools, and individual skills, the publisher cannot be responsible for any injuries, losses, and other damages that may result from the use of the information in this book.

If you have questions or comments about this book, please contact:
Lark Books, 67 Broadway, Asheville, NC 28801; (828) 253-0467.

Manufactured in China

ISBN-13: 978-1-60059-096-2

For information about custom editions, special sales, premium and corporate purchases, please contact Sterling Special Sales Department at (800) 805-5489 or specialsales@sterlingpub.com.

"Not on one strand are
all life's jewels strung."

— *William Morris*

TABLE OF CONTENTS

INTRODUCTION

I have been learning the craft of jewelry making for the past 20 years. I began making jewelry as a way to work with small objects that were easily transportable. When I first took up this craft, I would pack my bag of beads, wire, and needle-nose pliers and head to Spring Lake along the New Jersey shore and bead for hours.

Learning a craft, any craft, gives one a great sense of accomplishment and an inner approval that we are, in fact, creative.

This book has been made possible thanks to my large collection of beads and the inspiration I find designing jewelry among the many pieces in our craft shop, French General, in Los Angeles, California. French General's notion room is filled with old apothecary jars containing thousands of vintage glass beads, buttons, and baubles. Not only do we sell our beads to crafters who work with vintage materials, we also teach jewelry-making classes, where I enjoy sharing the knowledge I have gained over the many years I have been making jewelry.

French General stocks more than a ton of vintage glass beads from Japan, Italy, France, Germany, and the United States. By mixing these beads with a few newer notions we have created projects that will give you some ideas—and techniques—for creating your own vintage-inspired jewelry.

Because I am so inspired by life at the turn of the last century in rural France, I decided to design a line of jewelry for this book inspired by places that might have been a common part of life in the 1880s. The garden, the sea, the churchyard, or the vineyard...all can be seen through well-chosen colors.

I began designing these collections by arranging a palette for each chapter. Once I had my color scheme, the designs seemed to naturally form themselves. With a handful of simple beading techniques outlined in this book, you will be able to make any of the projects.

While browsing through these pages, find a silhouette or shape that challenges you to start designing, and then add your own creative stamp. Use this book as a guide to create your designs. If you can't find old green glass leaves embedded with wire, substitute green glass teardrop beads and use head pins for the wire. Learning to substitute beads early on is a great skill because all good beads run out eventually. I'll guide you in this with lots of options and sources for finding your own vintage treasures and reproductions.

Discovering Treasures

Imagine a basement full of old glass beads with shelves piled to the ceiling with cardboard boxes marked Made in Occupied Japan, Western Germany, or even Czechoslovakia.

I happened upon a basement just like this and many others in the late 1980s in New York City. I had started a line of vintage glass jewelry under my name, Kaari Meng Designs, and I was trying to find unusual materials to work with. My first great find was an old bead importer in a building on 37th Street, which was convenient for me since my studio was a block away.

Nearly every day I found myself wandering over to this bead warehouse to dig through the old stock. Covered in dust and grime, I opened every box I could reach and I almost always uncovered treasures. What I discovered was something I hadn't seen before—collections of old glass cabochons, beads, and buttons that had been carefully wrapped and then packed by the gross into boxes more than 60 years ago.

I started to organize my growing collection, first by type and then by color. The colors were cherry reds and Peking greens as well as turquoise blues and pinkish veined corals—almost garish colors. The color combinations seemed odd, but somehow fresh.

In 1992, I designed my first line of jewelry based on all of these old beads. Each collection featured a mix of the wonderful beads I had dug up, in addition to a sprinkling of reproduction beads made using old molds. Through this mixture of old and new I was able to manufacture my designs and broaden my collection, spreading my jewels around the country and as far away as Japan to specialty jewelry and clothing shops.

Defining Vintage

According to some bead traders, vintage beads are at least 50 years old. They can be previously used, but in the bead market, vintage beads are generally never-used stock. The beads have been sitting in bags and boxes in an old bead factory or warehouse somewhere, "ripening" with maturity. They are sought after because the designs are discontinued and represent a bygone era. Many Czech, German, Austrian, and Japanese vintage beads are still found on the market. Some consider beads that are 100 years or older antiques, which are extremely rare and often found on old clothes or in button tins at estate sales.

Most of the beads I have used in my designs over the years are vintage stock beads. I have found many in their original packaging in boxes packed by the kilo. Many road trips in our Grand Wagoneer to Providence, Rhode Island, in the early 1990s allowed me to collect the huge variety of beads that make up my jewelry today.

While old beads have a lovely charm, remember that newer varieties are a viable option. So whether you're creating with old or new beads, or a combination of the two, let your imagination guide you in creating your own vintage-inspired jewelry.

Kaari Meng

THE BASICS

Collecting beads takes perseverance and dedication. All sorts of beads pop up in the most unusual of places with prices ranging from extremely high to almost a steal.

Learning to buy beads you will actually use takes some time. Most of us do this by trial and error. If you are still learning what colors, shapes, and types of glass you like, study different pieces of jewelry. Go to museums, craft stores, bead shops, flea markets, antique shops, and thrift stores, or scour local garage sales on a Saturday morning. It's okay to be inspired by the creations of others; just remember that your designs should be unique and reflect your own style.

Collecting & Buying Vintage Beads

Buying old beads is a sensory experience—the smoothness of hand-blown glass beads, the weight of each bead, how they're strung together, the vivid colors, and, of course, the original packaging or labels. The physical characteristics are all clues that tell you a bit about the age of the beads and, if you are lucky, where they were made.

A long time ago I decided on the theory that the older the bead, the better. I eventually reevaluated things and changed my philosophy by collecting what appealed to me

most—just about anything that emulates nature, including hand-pulled leaves on wire, pressed glass with bird motifs, and hand-lacquered glass pearls.

Flea markets, bead shows, and bead shops are the best places to look at beads up close. Sometimes you'll find a great selection online; that is, once you're educated on what to look for. Again, keep an eye out for colors and shapes that strike you. If you love the look of hand-blown glass or lampwork beads, seek out artisans who make their own beads at craft or bead shows.

If you find yourself drawn to more organic colors and shapes, look for seashell, horn, coral, or wooden beads. And if your work lends itself to the ethnic, African or early American Indian trade beads are true beauties.

Once you have determined what you want to collect, buy as much as you can afford. Old glass is a great collectible and will go up in value, as will any craft with few masters. I always bought the whole box of beads or buttons when I could. If I couldn't afford the whole lot, I'd ask the dealer to hold onto the supply until I could afford the rest. This doesn't always work, but many dealers will often negotiate.

I have been slowly buying the stock for the past 10 years, and there are still more beads hidden in the importer's offices. Recently I received a call from the dealer, who told me she still had more than 12,000 of the beaded leaves. The amount of stock that was traded is just staggering.

Getting to know vendors and dealers is extremely important. In fact, without the great notion vendors I've found over the years, I would never have been able to continue to add to my collection. Letting dealers know exactly what I am looking for means they keep an eye out for me. I still get calls from vendors who have just come across basements full of old glass flowers, cranberry teardrops with wire loops, or crystal flower buttons still on their original cards.

Providence, Rhode Island is a great place to start digging for old glass beads. From the 1920s through the 1970s, Providence was the bead capital of the United States. Even today, you will find all sorts of bead importers listed in local phone books. Many of these warehouses will let you dig through their old stock and buy by the pound, but some have caught onto the trend of vintage materials and sell by the piece or even the dozen, which can add up fast.

Reproduction Beads

There are some beautiful reproduction beads made today. The majority is produced in the Czech Republic, where glassmaking is an age-old cottage industry. Reproductions are typically made by hand with original molds and colors, so they have the look and feel of old beads but are much more reasonably priced.

These beads are sold either by the strand or the gross. Many bead stores and Internet sites are now showing off these beautiful beads—shapes and colors that haven't been seen in more than 50 years. A good starting point is to do an online search for Czech beads, which should turn up a few dozen vendors that specialize in reproduction glass beads.

Color Inspiration

Les Fils d'É... PARIS

Vintage Hues

Some of the names used to identify bead colors at the turn of the last century up until the 1960s are rarely seen today. You know when you have come across a box of very old glass beads when they are marked "cerulean blue"—a wonderful shade reminiscent of a clear blue sky that is now called medium sapphire. Other wildly romantic hues listed by color include:

Red: cherry red, coral red, cranberry, crimson, dark ruby, garnet, Persian red, rose opal, vermilion

Orange: angel skin, carnelian, titian

Yellow: alabaster, butterscotch, citrine, jonquil, topaz

Green: beryl, jadeite, jasper, Peking, peridot, tourmaline

Blue: alexandrite, blue zircon, Capri, cornflower, indigo, Montana, turquoise

Violet: amethyst, claret, fuchsia, hyacinth, lavender, lilac, magenta

Black: black diamond, jet, onyx

Creating Palettes

Many of the glass colors used in beads more than 50 years ago are typically not seen today. The trends were different. Nature-inspired colors and gemstones, in addition to opaque, greasy, thick colors, were extremely popular.

Over the years, I have continued to seek out my favorite colors, like peridot greens and coral pinks. However, I have been won over by some more unusual colors like safranine red, opaque navy blue, and even chalk white.

Before you begin to design a piece of jewelry, it is important to come up with a palette, and the more original the better. Sometimes a collection of old postcards or a book of early sepia-tone photographs can inspire color combinations that will help you coordinate topaz beads with tiny glass pearl seed beads and just a touch of gold.

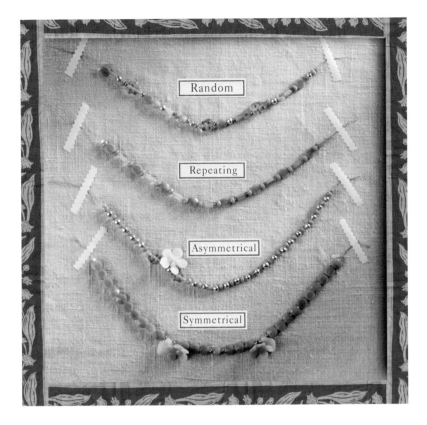

Design Inspiration

There are a few basic designs used in jewelry making, at least when making a necklace or bracelet. Basic design styles include the following:

Random—Random style is exactly that: a mixture of beads, patterns, and even color. This is a fabulous way to use your limited amount of old beads.

Repeating—This style forms a pattern of shapes (and color) and repeats it every inch or so.

Asymmetrical—Almost a lopsided approach. The two sides are set in an uneven pattern.

Symmetrical—These pieces are well proportioned and regular in form.

Types of Vintage Glass Beads

Bugle beads are small, tubular-shaped beads that vary in length from ⅛" to 2½". Like seed beads, they are usually used in very small work and seen in bead weaving designs.

Glass pearls are irregular round beads covered with a pearlized coating. Sometimes with a lead base, these pearls can be quite heavy and are a great first imitation of real pearls.

Embedded wire beads are made with a wire sunk into the glass that makes it easy to loop beads onto a chain or to use as pendants.

Glass rings are thin, fused glass rods that come in circular, oval, or square shapes. Made in Japan, most glass rings are extremely light-weight and fragile.

Mercury glass, also known as silvered glass, contains neither mercury nor silver. Made in France and Japan, these beads are hollow glass coated on the inside with a silvering formula. These beads are rare because they are delicate and tend to break easily.

Pressed-glass beads, some of the highest quality beads, are made by pressing glass into a mold. Many shapes can be made this way, including flowers and leaves. Patterns, such as the veins on the leaves, can also be imprinted onto the bead.

Nailhead beads are one-sided pressed-glass beads. Known as nailheads because they look like a hammered rivet or the head of a nail, these beads were made between 1920 and 1930 for the French garment industry.

Seed beads are small, round beads mainly used in beadwork. Each size is given a number and the larger the number, the smaller the bead. Most are 2mm or smaller.

Pliers & Cutters

I always have four basic tools on hand when designing jewelry: needle-nose pliers (A), preferably with a side cutter; flat-nose pliers (B); crimping pliers (C); and a pair of wire cutters (D).

If I am working on small pieces, I also like to have a smaller pair of flat-nose pliers and needle-nose pliers for wire wrapping and wire looping. The preferable needle-nose pliers have a side cutter, which makes wire looping a lot faster because you aren't constantly setting down your pliers to pick up the wire cutters.

Crimping pliers are specifically designed to crimp or crush tubular crimp beads and securely connect beading wires to clasps.

Flat-nose pliers are used to open and close jump rings as well as to crimp beads or tubes if you don't have crimping pliers.

Wire cutters are used to cut wire, eye pins, and head pins, in addition to most stringing materials including silk cord and elastic.

I store all of my tools, including a tube of glue, in a hemp roll that ties easily and keeps tools safe and clean. A tool roll allows you to travel easily with your tools at a moment's notice.

Adhesives

Since I began designing jewelry more than 20 years ago, I have been on the search for the perfect glue. I have tried almost everything and have found that each adhesive has its own makeup and consistency. Some are good for glass, others work well with metal, and some are best for more porous materials like mother-of-pearl.

Strong-hold glue is great for quick projects as it sets fairly quickly. This type of glue doesn't give you any time to reset or adjust a piece once glued. Two-part epoxies also work well, but there can be an element of wasted glue because the epoxies have to be mixed together on a glue card, and if you don't use it within a couple of minutes the glue hardens.

These days I am using a bonded cement glue. It dries pretty fast—within an hour—yet there is still time for moving items around. The secret to gluing is to cover the whole surface. So if you are gluing a charm onto a bezel, completely cover the back of the charm and then place it on the bezel. After gluing items, let them sit on a flat surface for at least an hour before you work on the piece or attach it to your design.

Once jewelry pieces have been glued and set, it is important to keep them away from extreme heat or moisture, as either of these elements will cause the glue to shift and may result in the piece falling off the bezel or charm.

When gluing a cushion-cut cabochon into a bezel, I prefer to fill the cup of the bezel with glue. Fill it to just below the top of the bezel and then set the cabochon into the setting. Too much glue becomes a mess by oozing out the sides, so start with a small amount. Remember, you can always add more.

Jewelry Findings

Jewelry findings are the component parts or materials that make up a piece of jewelry. There are all sorts of components that can be used to complement your jewelry designs. Many people choose to stick with one metal finish or color when designing, but you can create a charming, old-world look by mixing your metal and finding colors. Findings used throughout this book include:

Clasps: Connects the ends of a piece of jewelry together. Lobster clasps, spring rings, toggles, and swivel clasps are some of my favorites. (**A**)

Crimp beads: Tiny metal beads used to secure both ends of a necklace or bracelet strung with nylon cord. They also work well when stringing beads on elastic to hold the first bead in place.

Eye pins: Wire pins with a loop at one end used for linking beads or beaded links. Available in ½" to 3" lengths. I find the most useful size to be 1". (**B**)

Head pins: Wire with a flat head on one end, like a nail. Used to make bead dangles and to attach beads to loops in jewelry. The 1" length is usually sufficient. (**C**)

Jump rings: Small metal rings made out of wire, with a cut or split, used to attach charms, beads, clasps, and other findings onto a design. Typically, 3mm, 5mm, and 8mm jump rings are used. (**D**)

Ear wires: Small fish-hook-shaped wires used for earrings. The hook end passes through the pierced ear, while an ornament hangs from the opposite end. The French wire is also a popular earring finding; both of these ear wires can have small bezels or stampings soldered on in order to hold a cabochon. (**E**)

Split rings: Similar in size and shape to jump rings but resist stretching because they cannot be opened.

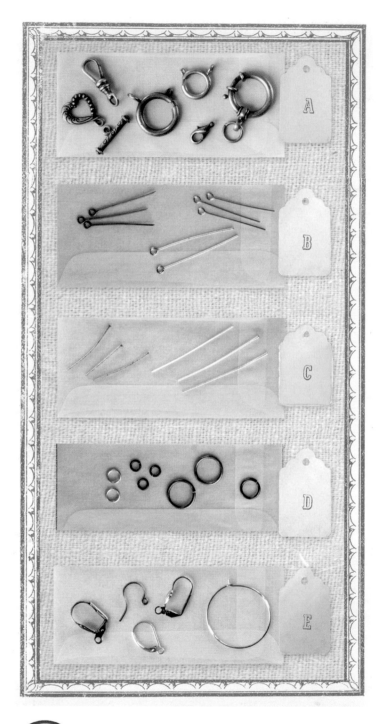

Castings

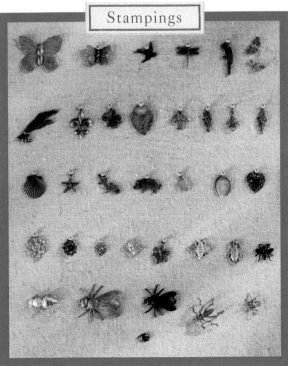

Stampings

Metal Findings

In costume jewelry the castings, charms, and heavier bezels are typically brass or a white metal similar to pewter. Almost any hard item can be set into a mold and cast.

Over the years, I have collected an enormous amount of charms from flea markets that I have sunk into a mold and made castings out of. Most metals, and some glass, can be used as a model to make a mold. If you have an old charm or glass button you would like to reproduce, find a local casting company and ask to have a sample mold made. Sample molds are usually rubber and can cast up to 24 pieces. If you want to have more pieces made and don't need to see a sample, ask for the production mold and you will be able to cast as many as you like.

There are all sorts of plating colors you can choose from. Pewter-ox, brass-ox, and dark copper-ox are oxidized colors that have a slight blackening or antique wash on them. Silver, bright gold (also known as Hamilton gold), and copper plate are all shinier colors that tend to oxidize naturally over time. By plating your castings or stampings, you are giving them a wash of color and sealing the raw metal so that, hopefully, the color won't change too quickly. You can also try rubbing a mix of black and brown acrylic paint onto raw brass pieces, wiping off after 30 seconds, and then sealing with a lacquer to hold the color.

Stampings are very thin sheets of brass imprinted with dies to produce cutouts like charms or filigree. Stampings have become popular with scrapbookers now, but in the 1930s and '40s, they were the staple of costume jewelry. Many of the filigree pieces were beaded using a thin-gauge plated wire to sew small beads onto the brass stamping, referred to as cagework.

GLASS-IMITATION
STONES
SQUARES

Bezels

Bezels are the metal frames or disks into which cabochons are set. There are flat-back bezels, which cabochons are glued onto, and prong bezels, which have a deeper cup that accommodates cushion-back cabochons, also known as cushion-cut bezels. After gluing the cabochon into a prong bezel, set aside to dry for at least an hour and then use flat-nose pliers to fold down the prongs. This can also be done by pressing the prongs into a flat surface—like a worktable—and rolling forward softly.

Before I have my bezels plated, I have a ring or two soldered onto the metal so that I can attach the bezel to a piece of chain using a jump ring. Without the rings soldered on, the bezel can only be glued down to a flat surface, which can limit your designs.

Chains

Using chains in jewelry is a great way to break up a heavily beaded necklace or link a charm bracelet. A good rule of thumb is to find a chain link size you enjoy wearing, and chances are you'll enjoy working with it. Large links can end up looking too chunky while small links can be problematic with jump rings and other wire—not to mention taxing on your eyes!

There used to be a handful of chain manufacturers in Providence that were still working with vintage tools to create great old-looking chains, but these companies are becoming scarce because the cost of manufacturing has become too high. The chains I use are raw brass; I then plate them to create a warm gold color.

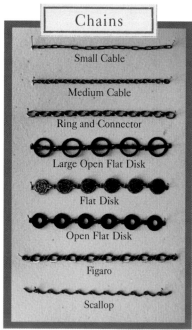

Small Cable

Medium Cable

Ring and Connector

Large Open Flat Disk

Flat Disk

Open Flat Disk

Figaro

Scallop

Stringing Materials

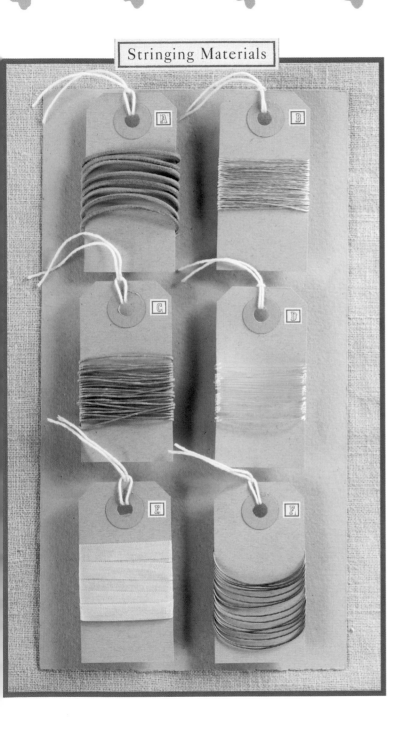

Stringing Materials

Leather cord: Typically available in a couple of different widths and finishes. You can knot the ends to finish or use a crimping clasp, which has the crimp bead set into the clasp. (**A**)

Silk cord: Silk makes one of the nicest drapes on a necklace, and there is nothing smoother or softer. Silk has been the traditional stringing material for centuries. Many silk cords come with a thin needle that allows you to bead the tiniest of seed beads. Silk cord is available in many colors and can be finished with a triple knot and a bead cap, the first and last finding you string onto your piece. (**B**)

Wax cord or hemp: Natural wax cord or hemp is easy to thread and resists twisting or knotting and is a great material to make long necklaces with multiple charms because it doesn't appear too heavy. It can be finished with crimping beads and a clasp or knotted at the ends. (**C**)

Elastic cord: Strong, clear elastic cord comes in a variety of colors and widths. Elastic can be finished by triple knotting and securing with a spot of glue or by using a crimp bead and clasp. (**D**)

Ribbon: Ribbons or other fibers are a great way to add texture and design to your jewelry. Use ribbons as a base to string charms onto or to close necklaces or bracelets. Small bits of old fibers look great woven into chain or tied onto jump rings. Ribbons can be finished by crimping a ribbon clasp onto each end. (**E**)

Nylon cord: Nylon-coated wire is great for basic bead stringing. It is available in either a three- or seven-strand diameter. Nylon cord is finished by using a crimp bead and split ring. (**F**)

Standard Necklace Lengths

High Neck 14"

Choker 16"

Princess 18"

Matinee 20 – 24"

Opera 32"

Rope 40 – 45"

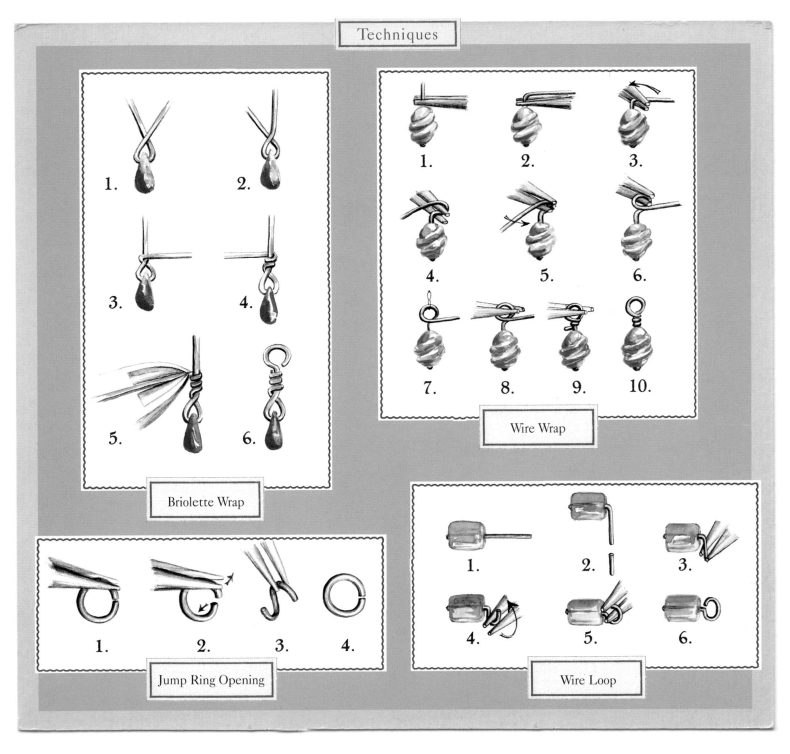

Techniques

1. 2. 3. 4. 5. 6.

Briolette Wrap

1. 2. 3. 4. 5. 6. 7. 8. 9. 10.

Wire Wrap

1. 2. 3. 4.

Jump Ring Opening

1. 2. 3. 4. 5. 6.

Wire Loop

LA MER

Turquoise seas, coral shells, and white sand have been a constant inspiration in my jewelry designs. Collecting estate jewelry from the south of France has always given me a great color palette reminiscent of carefree jaunts to another part of the world.

When collecting old glass to design a seaside piece, look for coral and turquoise glass, as well as seashells and mother-of-pearl that can be drilled for stringing. Before drilling, leave the pieces in the sun to air out any smells or to bleach any discoloration. After a couple of days, scrub lightly with a small brush and then, using a Dremel drill with a fine diamond bit, make a hole. Look for old brass starfishes, seahorses, and boats on costume jewelry to add to your designs.

MON ÂME SE SITUE

AU SOLEIL

CONVERTIBLE NECKLACE

MATERIALS

Beads: 3x5mm faceted donut glass (20)

Beads: 7mm glass (10)

Cable chain: 6mm brass-plated (20")

Charms (4–5)

Disk chain: 9mm brass-plated (10 disks)

Disks: 9mm mother-of-pearl (10)

Eye pins: 1" 22-gauge brass-plated (34)

Jump rings: 5mm brass-plated (2)

Jump rings: 8mm brass-plated (4–6)

Spring ring clasp: 30mm brass-plated

TOOLS

Flat-nose pliers

Jeweler's glue

Needle-nose pliers

Wire cutters

I have been making this same necklace for more than 15 years, never tiring of its simplicity. The beauty of this piece is that it can be worn so many different ways. As one long strand, all the charms mirror a collection of tiny souvenirs; worn short, with just a single charm, it could pass for an heirloom piece.

❈ INSTRUCTIONS ❈

Glue mother-of-pearl disks onto disk chain. Set aside at least one hour to dry. Meanwhile, cut cable chain into twenty 1" pieces. Thread 7mm glass beads onto eye pins and link onto one end of chain. Thread 3x5mm glass donut beads onto eye pins and link onto opposite end of chain.

Once pearl disks are dry, connect one disk between each 3x5mm glass donut bead. Continue this pattern: one bead, one link of chain, one donut bead, one disk, and one donut bead, until you have 34" length of beaded chain.

Connect spring ring clasp to either end of chain using 5mm jump ring. Connect charms using 8mm jump rings.

DESIGN TIP

MAKING YOUR OWN CHARMS

Making charms out of found materials or vintage glass is another way to add personality to your jewelry. Start with a large base or brass setting and add cabochons, beads, or mother-of-pearl disks. The right cement glue is especially important because charms will take a little more wear and tear than other pieces, especially if they are on a charm bracelet.

SCALLOPED CHAIN NECKLACE

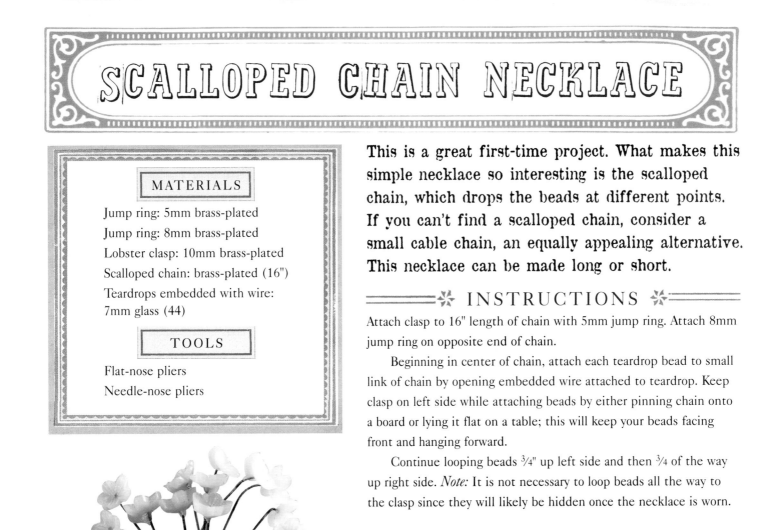

MATERIALS

Jump ring: 5mm brass-plated
Jump ring: 8mm brass-plated
Lobster clasp: 10mm brass-plated
Scalloped chain: brass-plated (16")
Teardrops embedded with wire:
7mm glass (44)

TOOLS

Flat-nose pliers
Needle-nose pliers

This is a great first-time project. What makes this simple necklace so interesting is the scalloped chain, which drops the beads at different points. If you can't find a scalloped chain, consider a small cable chain, an equally appealing alternative. This necklace can be made long or short.

❊ INSTRUCTIONS ❊

Attach clasp to 16" length of chain with 5mm jump ring. Attach 8mm jump ring on opposite end of chain.

Beginning in center of chain, attach each teardrop bead to small link of chain by opening embedded wire attached to teardrop. Keep clasp on left side while attaching beads by either pinning chain onto a board or lying it flat on a table; this will keep your beads facing front and hanging forward.

Continue looping beads ¾" up left side and then ¾ of the way up right side. *Note:* It is not necessary to loop beads all the way to the clasp since they will likely be hidden once the necklace is worn.

FAVORITES

EMBEDDED WIRE GLASS

Glass drops embedded with wire were made in the 1920s as an alternative to threading each bead with a head pin. The wire embedded into the glass can either be straight, which was used for glass floral arranging, or already looped, which was mainly used in jewelry making.

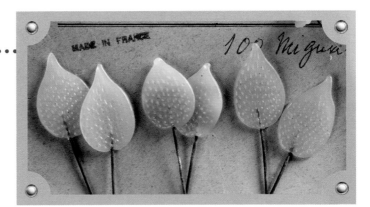

MOTHER-OF-PEARL PINS

MATERIALS

Bar pin: 1" brass
Bezel: 9x7mm
Brass charm: seashell
Cabochon: 9x7mm
Cabochons: 3mm (23)
Cabochons: 5mm (2)
Cabochons: 8mm (4)
Crystal: 14x5mm
Crystals: 2mm (5)
Disk: 25mm mother-of-pearl

TOOLS

Jeweler's glue

A large button or mother-of-pearl disk serves as the base for anything that can be added on top of these pins. Look for old teething rings, gaming chips, or wooden nickels—all make great bases for this pin project. It's almost like making a large charm, only there is a pin base glued to the back of the mother-of-pearl disk.

CORAL SEASHELL PIN

❉ INSTRUCTIONS ❉

Glue bar pin onto back of mother-of-pearl disk; let dry completely. Lay out collection of beads and cabochons on mother-of-pearl base for positioning. Glue on brass seashell charm with open side up, then fit other cabochons in and around it.

Once you have glued larger pieces down, start adding smaller pieces and layering cabochons on pin.

BLUE OPAL PIN

❉ INSTRUCTIONS ❉

Glue bar pin onto back of mother-of-pearl disk and let dry completely. Lay out collection of beads and cabochons on mother-of-pearl disk for positioning. Glue blue opal cabochons around edge of pin. Glue high-dome cabochon to center of pin. Pour small amount of jeweler's glue around center cabochon and gently fill in with seed beads. *Note:* Be careful not to let any seed beads overlap each other; there should only be a single layer of seed beads.

MATERIALS

Bar pin: 1" brass
Cabochons: 3mm blue opal (9)
Cabochons: 8x6mm blue opal (9)
Disk: 25mm mother-of-pearl
High-dome cabochon: 15x15mm pressed-glass
Seed beads: silver-lined blue (100)

TOOLS

Jeweler's glue

STRETCH TURQUOISE BRACELETS

MATERIALS

BRACELET NO. 1:

Beads with large holes: 6mm (30)

String: .7mm elastic (10")

BRACELET NO. 2:

Nailhead beads: 6mm (27)

String: .7mm elastic (10")

BRACELET NO. 3:

Beads with large holes: 6mm (30)

String: .7mm elastic (10")

BRACELET NO. 4:

Beads: 12mm square (11)

String: .7mm elastic (10")

TOOLS

Quick-drying adhesive

Hands down, the stretch turquoise bracelets are the easiest project in this book. The secret to these bracelets is finding beads with holes large enough to thread through elastic string. Wear up to a dozen of these bracelets for a great look. Adding words out of glass letters is a fun way to send a message, or spell out the names of your children or pets.

❖ INSTRUCTIONS ❖

Triple knot one end of elastic string. Thread beads onto elastic for 6½". Once you have a comfortable size that fits your wrist snuggly, tie ends of elastic in three knots. Add a drop of adhesive to cover knots; set aside to dry.

DESIGN TIP

CRIMP SECURELY

The stretch bracelet will last longer if you take the time to knot the ends securely three times and then let the glue dry completely. Another trick is to add a crimp bead before you start beading; this will hold the first bead in place. You can also add a crimp bead at the end of the bracelet and then knot.

Grands Magasins du Louvre - Paris
COMPTOIR DES INDIENNES N° 17
OXFORD

Largeur 80

PRODUIT GARANTI PUR

This imported article of
synthetic phenolic resin
was manufactured by a
foreign concern in no
wise connected with the
Bakelite Corp. and
American corpor.

MADE IN CZECHOSLOVAKIA

CORAL CHARM BRACELET

MATERIALS

Bezels: brass-plated to fit glass cabochons (22)

Cable chain: 5mm brass-plated (7")

Cabochons: to fit bezels (22)

Jump ring: 5mm brass-plated

Jump ring: 8mm brass-plated

Jump rings: 3mm brass-plated (22)

Spring ring clasp: 12mm brass-plated

TOOLS

Flat-nose pliers

Jeweler's glue

❋ INSTRUCTIONS ❋

Attach clasp with 5mm jump ring to end of chain. Attach 8mm jump ring to opposite end of chain. Lay out chain with clasp on left side of table so that beads will hang forward and straight.

Glue each cabochon into bezel to create charms; let dry. While drying, lay out pattern of elements along chain. *Note:* Keep in mind that heavier charms are usually better balanced in the center. Work your way out from there, keeping the balance of shapes in mind.

When charms are dry, begin attaching them with 3mm jump rings. Add charms as you find them or add to bracelet at once.

CHARM EARRINGS

❋ INSTRUCTIONS ❋

Glue 14x10mm coral cabochon to 14x10mm brass bezel, 10mm coral cabochon to 12mm disk chain link, 6mm coral cabochon to 7mm disk chain link, and coral nailhead bead to earring finding; set aside to dry.

Add second layer to 6mm coral cabochon by gluing another coral nailhead bead on top. Once all settings are dry, connect 14x10mm bezel to 12mm disk using oval jump ring. Connect 12mm disk chain link to 7mm disk chain link, and finally, 7mm disk chain link to earring finding. Repeat steps to make second earring.

MATERIALS

Bezels: 14x10mm brass-ox plated (2)

Cabochons: 6mm coral (2)

Cabochons: 10mm coral (2)

Cabochons: 14x10mm coral glass (2)

Disk chain links: 7mm brass-ox plated (2)

Disk chain links: 12mm brass-ox plated (2)

Jump rings: 4mm brass-ox plated oval (6)

Nailhead beads: 5mm glass coral (4)

Star earring findings: brass-ox plated (2)

TOOLS

Flat-nose pliers

Jeweler's glue

MOTHER-OF-PEARL CHARM BRACELET

MATERIALS

Bezels: 15mm, 18mm, 8x10mm, 9x9mm 10x13mm, 11mm copper-ox plated

Cable chain: 8mm brass-ox plated (7½")

Cabochon: 5mm pink crystal

Cabochon: 8x10mm coral glass

Cabochon: 10x13mm coral

Disk chain link: 9mm, 12mm brass-ox plated

Disks: 12mm, 15mm, 18mm mother-of-pearl; 9mm mother-of-pearl (4)

Fish beads: 5x11mm glass (2)

Flower: 20mm mother-of-pearl

Head pins: 1" brass-ox plated (3)

Jump ring: 9mm brass-plated

Jump rings: 5mm brass-ox plated (12)

Nailhead bead: 5mm white glass

Pearl drops embedded with wire: 15x7mm glass (5)

Pearl seashells with embedded wire: 18x20mm glass (3)

Spring ring clasp: 12mm brass-ox plated

Square disk: 5x5mm, 9x9mm mother-of-pearl

TOOLS

Flat-nose pliers

Jeweler's glue

Needle-nose pliers

Wire cutters

❈ INSTRUCTIONS ❈

Glue cabochons into their respective bezels; set aside to dry. *Note:* Some of these charms are glued onto the cabochons, so glue the first layer down and once dry, glue the second layer.

Open 5mm jump ring and connect clasp to one end of cable chain. Connect 9mm jump ring to opposite end. Lay clasp on left side and attach charms at every large cable link using 5mm jump rings. Cut embedded wire glass beads and loop directly onto chain.

DESIGN TIP

MIXING SHADES OF ONE COLOR

Most jewelry is made with a great mixture of color, but consider using only one basic color and variations of the hue. Whether borrowing colors from nature or going to a hardware store and looking at the shades on a paint card, try to choose a monochromatic color scheme to design a piece of jewelry in one palette. This very simple technique allows jewelry to have a richness that is hard to achieve with multiple colors.

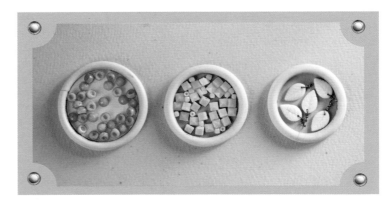

LE MARCHE

HAND PICKED, INCREDIBLY DELICIOUS FRESH FRUIT

> " When I sound the fairy call,
> gather here in silent meeting,
> Chin to knee on the orchard wall,
> cooled with dew and cherries eating.
> Merry, merry, take a cherry, mine
> are sounder, mine are rounder,
> Mine are sweeter for the eater,
> when the dews fall, and you'll be
> fairies all. "
>
> —*Emily Dickinson*

Walking through a morning market in France is a feast for the eyes. The ripe red tomatoes, cherries, and apples sit right alongside bundles of apple blossom branches and sunflowers. Taking inspiration from the bright, fresh colors of the organic market in St. Antonin-Noble-Val, I have designed some whimsical pieces that use both new and old glass fruit charms.

Glass fruit often comes randomly strung, so you get a bit of everything when you buy one strand. Search for the great reproduction fruit and vegetable charms being made today, or look for an old necklace and cut off the charms to use in one of your jewelry pieces.

RED FLOWER SWAG NECKLACE

MATERIALS

Cable chain: 4mm brass-ox plated (24")

Faceted beads: 4mm red glass (24)

Flowers with embedded wire: 17x17mm red glass (6)

Head pins: 1" brass-ox plated (33)

Jump ring: 5mm brass-ox plated

Jump rings: 8mm brass-ox plated (2)

Round beads: 4mm coral (15)

Spring ring clasp: 12mm brass-ox plated

TOOLS

Needle-nose pliers

This necklace incorporates cherry red and orange coral glass beads, along with vintage glass flowers on wire. The clasp connects in the front in order to let the "tail" dangle off the necklace.

INSTRUCTIONS

Cut 2" of chain for swag that will hang off clasp. Thread coral bead onto embedded wire of flower; cut and loop onto chain every fourth link of swag. Between flowers, thread coral bead onto head pin; cut and loop onto chain so there is a pattern of flower, coral bead, flower, coral bead, etc. Connect end of chain to clasp using 5mm jump ring. Attach remaining flower to jump ring.

Thread remaining beads onto head pins; cut and loop directly onto every fourth link on 22" chain. Attach fourteen beads per side.

Attach large 8mm jump ring and clasp to one end of chain and remaining 8mm jump ring to opposite end.

RED FLOWER EARRINGS

INSTRUCTIONS

Cut chain into two 1½" pieces. Cut and loop flowers by directly attaching onto chain at second and sixth link, approximately ½" apart.

Thread coral glass beads through head pins; cut and loop directly onto remaining links of chain to create cluster around the flowers.

Open ear wire and attach to end of chain. Repeat steps to make second earring.

MATERIALS

Beads: 7mm coral glass (12)

Cable chain: 3mm brass-ox plated (3")

Ear wires: brass-ox plated (2)

Flowers with embedded wire: 17x17mm red glass (4)

Head pins: 1" brass-ox plated (12)

TOOLS

Needle-nose pliers

Wire cutters

Player's Cigarettes

APPLE BLOSSOM BRACELET

MATERIALS

Apples embedded with wire: glass (5)

Bezels: 8mm brass (2)

Bezels: 14x14mm brass-ox plated (3)

Cabochons: 8mm garnet (2)

Cabochons: 12x12mm jonquil glass (3)

Flowers: brass (2); red glass (5)

Flowers embedded with wire: yellow glass (4)

Headpins: 1" brass-ox plated (20)

Jump ring: 8mm brass-ox plated

Jump rings: 3mm brass-ox plated (7)

Ladybugs: red glass (6)

Leaves: green glass (10)

Spring ring clasp: 12mm brass-ox plated

TOOLS

Jeweler's glue

Needle-nose pliers

Wire cutters

This bracelet reminds me of the festive glass used during the 1930s. The reds and yellows blend together with some help from the green glass leaves. I also used some small crystal cabochons for a bit of sparkle.

❀ INSTRUCTIONS ❀

Glue jonquil and garnet cabochons onto bezels; set aside to dry. Cut glass apples and glass flowers embedded with wire; loop directly onto chain every third link. Thread ladybugs, leaves, and red flowers onto head pins; cut and loop directly onto chain on every other link. Connect brass flowers onto chain with 3mm jump rings.

When cabochons have finished drying, open 3mm jump ring and attach to chain. *Note:* Use these cabochons as fill-in pieces and sprinkle throughout bracelet where needed.

Attach clasp to one end of chain using remaining 3mm jump ring. Open 8mm jump ring and attach to opposite end of chain.

DESIGN TIP

PRETTY AS A NECKLACE

Sometimes a charm bracelet is too fragile to wear on your wrist. If you have an extra 10" of chain lying around, make a bracelet extension. Add a small clasp with a jump ring onto both ends of the chain, and then connect the clasps to either end of the charm bracelet—within minutes you will have an instant necklace.

CHERRY GLASS BRACELET

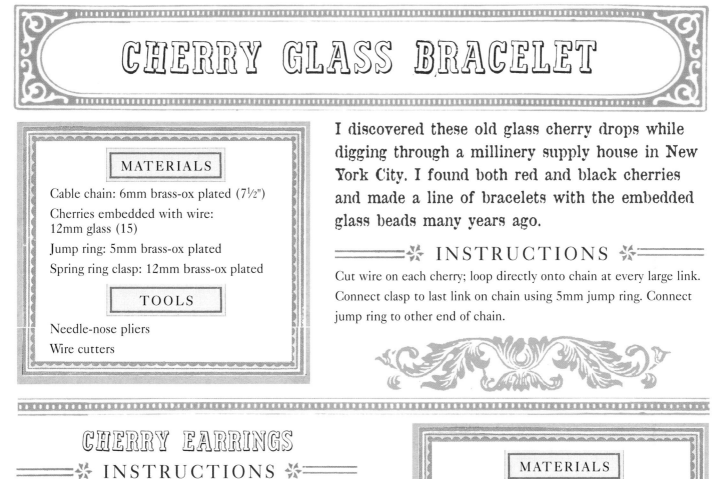

MATERIALS

Cable chain: 6mm brass-ox plated (7½")

Cherries embedded with wire: 12mm glass (15)

Jump ring: 5mm brass-ox plated

Spring ring clasp: 12mm brass-ox plated

TOOLS

Needle-nose pliers

Wire cutters

I discovered these old glass cherry drops while digging through a millinery supply house in New York City. I found both red and black cherries and made a line of bracelets with the embedded glass beads many years ago.

❈ INSTRUCTIONS ❈

Cut wire on each cherry; loop directly onto chain at every large link. Connect clasp to last link on chain using 5mm jump ring. Connect jump ring to other end of chain.

CHERRY EARRINGS

❈ INSTRUCTIONS ❈

Cut cable chain into four ½" pieces. Cut and loop glass cherry onto end of each piece of chain.

Open 8mm jump ring and loop onto one piece of chain with cherry and through hole in glass leaf: close jump ring. Open 5mm jump ring and thread through remaining cherry on chain, and then thread on 8mm jump ring, last cherry, and green glass ring. Once drop is made, connect remaining 5mm jump ring to top of glass ring and then to ear wire. Repeat steps to make second earring.

MATERIALS

Cable chain: 3mm brass-ox plated (3")

Cherries embedded with wire: 12mm glass (6)

Ear wires: brass-ox plated (2)

Jump rings: 5mm brass-ox plated (4)

Jump rings: 8mm brass-ox plated (2)

Leaves: 30x17mm green glass (2)

Rings: 12mm green glass (2)

TOOLS

Needle-nose pliers

Wire cutters

VIEILLE

SUMMER FRUIT NECKLACE

MATERIALS

Apples embedded with wire:
10mm glass (6)

Beads: 4mm coral glass (60)

Beads: 8mm amber glass (20)

Briolettes: 7x5mm fuchsia glass (11)

Buttons: 9mm coral glass (20)

Coin beads: 12mm green glass (5)

Eye pins: 1" gold-plated (55)

Jump ring: 10mm brass-ox plated

Jump rings: 3mm gold-plated (36)

Jump rings: 5mm gold-plated (12)

Leaves embedded with wire: 9mm
green glass (20)

Lemons: 10mm glass (10)

Rings: 14mm green glass (6)

Spring ring clasp: 25mm brass-ox plated

Wire: 24-gauge gold-plated (36")

TOOLS

Needle-nose pliers

Wire cutters

This necklace features all sorts of vintage glass fruit and fruit-inspired beads. You can substitute fruit glass beads for solid beads in fruity colors, and then add small leaves to make them look freshly picked off the tree.

❊ INSTRUCTIONS ❊

Thread two coral beads onto eye pin; cut and loop end. Thread amber bead onto eye pin; cut and loop onto coral beads. Continue this pattern: two coral beads, one amber bead, two coral beads, one amber bead ending with two coral beads. Attach green glass ring using 5mm jump ring. Attach another 5mm jump ring to glass ring and repeat pattern; attach green coin bead with eye pin. Continue alternating glass rings and coin beads between patterns until 32" strand is made.

Cut and loop wire on each apple. *Note:* Use head pin if you don't have apples embedded with wire. Attach each apple to green glass rings using 5mm jump ring.

To connect briolettes: Cut 2" piece of gold wire and, using briolette wrap technique, wire wrap briolettes and attach directly onto linked chain of beads. *Note:* The briolettes act as the berries dripping off the chain.

Attach coral glass buttons and lemons using 3mm jump rings. Cut and wire leaves directly onto linked chain of beads. Between each glass ring, evenly distribute four coral glass buttons, two lemons, two leaves, and two briolettes.

Once finished hanging beaded fruit off chain of beads, connect clasp using 5mm jump ring; attach 10mm jump ring to opposite end of necklace.

PRODUCE OF FRANCE

CHARLES RAY

VASES EN POTERIE POUR FLEURS ET ARBUSTES

Vases bruts sans pied ni anses	Vases vernis vert avec pied et anses	Plateaux vernis vert partout	Vases coniques vernis vert
Nᵒˢ 1 à 15	Nᵒˢ 16 à 30	Nᵒˢ 31 à 40	Nᵒˢ 41 à 47

(15 grandeurs)   (15 grandeurs)   (10 grandeurs)   (7 grandeurs)

FRUIT WATCH BRACELET

MATERIALS

Apples embedded with wire: 6mm glass (2)
Bananas embedded with wire: 6x18mm glass (6)
Cable chain: 5mm brass-ox plated (7½")
Grapes: 9x14mm glass (4)
Jump ring: 8mm brass-ox plated
Jump rings: 5mm brass-ox plated (13)
Pears embedded with wire: 9x14mm glass (10)
Ribbon: 5mm silk (6")
Spring ring clasp: 12mm brass-ox plated
Watch face: 25mm

TOOLS

Needle-nose pliers
Wire cutters

This is a fun twist on an old idea. The watch face is actually tied to the charm bracelet using bits of ribbon. The ribbon gives the bracelet more texture and the watch face makes it functional.

INSTRUCTIONS

Cut chain in half. Cut and loop all glass fruit with embedded wire. Attach 5mm jump ring to side hole in each grape.

Attach cluster of fruit—grape, apple, and pear—to a second 5mm jump ring. Connect fruit cluster to second link on chain. Continue assembling fruit clusters—apple, banana, and pear—on 5mm jump rings. Connect to every other link on the chain.

Attach four clusters of fruit to each piece of chain. Cut ribbon in half and thread through link on the bottom of watch face. Thread same length of ribbon through last link on chain. Repeat on opposite side and tie both ribbon ends into tight knot so watch face is connected to chain with clustered fruit.

Open remaining 5mm jump ring and connect clasp to opposite end of chain. Open 8mm jump ring and connect to opposite end of chain.

DESIGN TIP

WEARING WATCH CHARMS

I like the idea of wearing time, but I prefer to think of the watch face as a charm rather than the main focus of the piece. There are all sorts of wonderful gold watches in antique shops, or maybe even in your own jewelry box. Consider removing an old watch face from its strap and using it as a charm.

BERRY CLUSTER NECKLACE

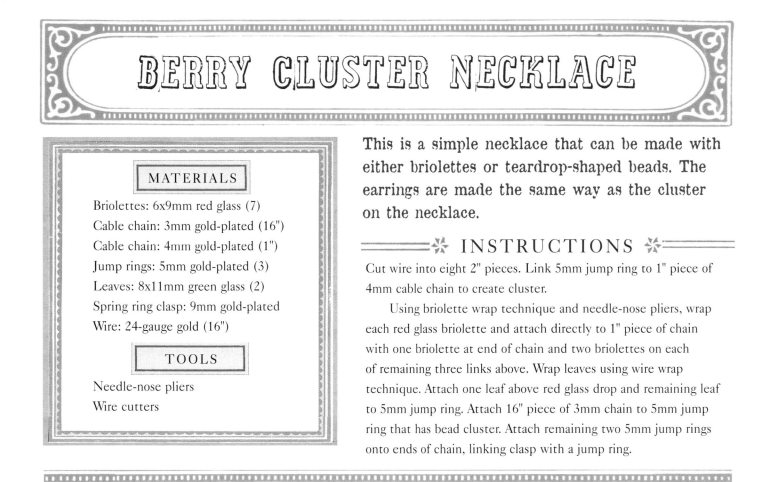

MATERIALS

Briolettes: 6x9mm red glass (7)

Cable chain: 3mm gold-plated (16")

Cable chain: 4mm gold-plated (1")

Jump rings: 5mm gold-plated (3)

Leaves: 8x11mm green glass (2)

Spring ring clasp: 9mm gold-plated

Wire: 24-gauge gold (16")

TOOLS

Needle-nose pliers

Wire cutters

This is a simple necklace that can be made with either briolettes or teardrop-shaped beads. The earrings are made the same way as the cluster on the necklace.

❖ INSTRUCTIONS ❖

Cut wire into eight 2" pieces. Link 5mm jump ring to 1" piece of 4mm cable chain to create cluster.

Using briolette wrap technique and needle-nose pliers, wrap each red glass briolette and attach directly to 1" piece of chain with one briolette at end of chain and two briolettes on each of remaining three links above. Wrap leaves using wire wrap technique. Attach one leaf above red glass drop and remaining leaf to 5mm jump ring. Attach 16" piece of 3mm chain to 5mm jump ring that has bead cluster. Attach remaining two 5mm jump rings onto ends of chain, linking clasp with a jump ring.

CLUSTER EARRINGS

❖ INSTRUCTIONS ❖

Using briolette wrap technique and needle-nose pliers, wrap each red glass briolette and attach directly to 1" piece of chain, placing one briolette at end of chain and two briolettes on each of remaining three links above. Attach glass leaves in the same manner. Attach top of chain to ear wire. Repeat steps to make second earring.

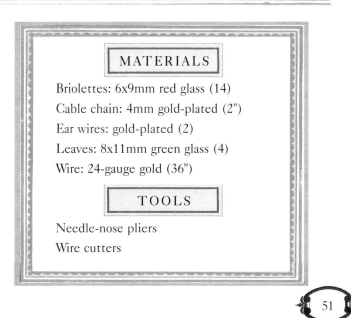

MATERIALS

Briolettes: 6x9mm red glass (14)

Cable chain: 4mm gold-plated (2")

Ear wires: gold-plated (2)

Leaves: 8x11mm green glass (4)

Wire: 24-gauge gold (36")

TOOLS

Needle-nose pliers

Wire cutters

LE CIRQUE

The traveling circus, in its heyday from 1880 to 1920, featured human endurance and skill as well as animal acts involving chimpanzees, seals, and elephants. A day at the circus in Bordeaux at turn-of-the-last-century France was filled with color and sights to behold. The circus was typically set up in a large tent with smaller tents outside that held the sideshows.

Taking inspiration from the colors and patterns found at an old circus, I have designed a handful of pieces that might have been worn by carnival characters and could have been the souvenirs one might have won at the penny arcade games.

PORTE MONNAIE LE TANNEUR
SANS COUTURE

Solidité
Incomparable

MARQUE DÉPOSÉE

Système
Breveté

HAND-KNOTTED LARIAT

MATERIALS

Beads: 4mm green glass (60)
Beads: 10mm carnival glass (4)
Charms: brass (8)
Coin beads: 8mm amber glass (6)
Heart beads: 6mm ruby glass (14)
Leaf beads: 9mm green glass (12)
Pearl beads: 10mm glass (4)
Pressed-flower beads: 12x8mm pink glass (12)
Seed beads 2mm bronze glass (24)
Side-drilled teardrop beads: 12mm pink glass (6)
Waxed cord (48")

TOOLS

Needle-nose pliers
Scissors

This necklace can be made with a variety of stringing materials. I've chosen a waxed hemp cord, but you may want to use a leather or silk cord. This necklace lends itself to all the scraps and bits left over from other designs.

INSTRUCTIONS

Tie a triple knot at one end of waxed cord and string two 4mm glass beads onto cord. Add pressed-flower bead and another two 4mm glass beads. Tie knot right after 4mm beads to hold them in place. Tie a second knot approximately ½" down the cord.

Bead in any desired pattern, keeping balance and color in mind. String one, two, three, or four beads onto cord, then tie another knot to hold them in place. Thread on a brass charm every 3" and secure with a knot. Continue desired pattern until you reach end of waxed cord. *Note:* If the end tip of the cord starts to fray and it becomes too difficult to thread the beads, make a slanted cut with scissors; this will give you a new tip to work with.

Once you've finished stringing and have knotted all beads onto cord, triple knot end to ensure that beads stay in place.

DESIGN TIP

ADDING MORE CHARMS

After you've finished stringing and knotting all of your beads onto a waxed cord, try threading a head pin through a couple of teardrop or elongated beads and looping the wire around the waxed cord, between two beads. This creates a garland effect that highlights your collection of lucky charms.

CHARM WATCH NECKLACE

MATERIALS

Bezel: 12x17mm brass ox-plated

Bezel: 15mm brass ox-plated

Cable chain: 6mm brass oxplated (38")

Cabochon: 12x17mm

Cabochon: 15mm

Charm: brass

Floral beads embedded with wire: 12x18 (17)

Jump ring: 5mm brass ox-plated

Jump rings: 3mm brass ox-plated (17)

Jump rings: 8mm brass ox-plated (3–4)

Swivel watch clasp: brass ox-plated

Watch face

TOOLS

Jeweler's glue

Needle-nose pliers

Wire cutters

I designed this necklace to look like an old circus barker's timepiece. The floral beads dripping off the sides of the chain could be almost any bead, but I liked the way the flowers gave the piece a whimsical look.

❋ INSTRUCTIONS ❋

Glue cabochons into their respective bezels; set aside to dry. Cut chain in half. Attach swivel watch clasp to one end of chain using 5mm jump ring. Attach 8mm jump ring to opposite end of chain, and then link ends together.

To create beaded drops: working with floral embedded beads with wire, cut and loop each wire. Attach directly onto chain or use 3mm jump rings. Either count links in chain and attach bead approximately every twelve links, or simply judge placement with your eyes and attach beads every 1½". *Note:* Try to keep the bead count even on both sides.

Attach brass charm, watch face, and additional charms as desired using 8mm jump rings. If desired, fold necklace in half and attach 8mm jump ring onto swivel clasp at back to create a shorter necklace with charms.

FAVORITES

HAND-PAINTED CABOCHONS

Throughout the 1930s and '40s cabochons were made out of pressed glass and then hand-painted to enhance their detail. Finding these old cabochons with their painting details still intact can be quite a challenge. If you look for pieces that were carefully wrapped and haven't been exposed to the elements you might be able to still enjoy their original expressions or colors.

A

B

C

D

E

COLLECTION OF BRACELETS

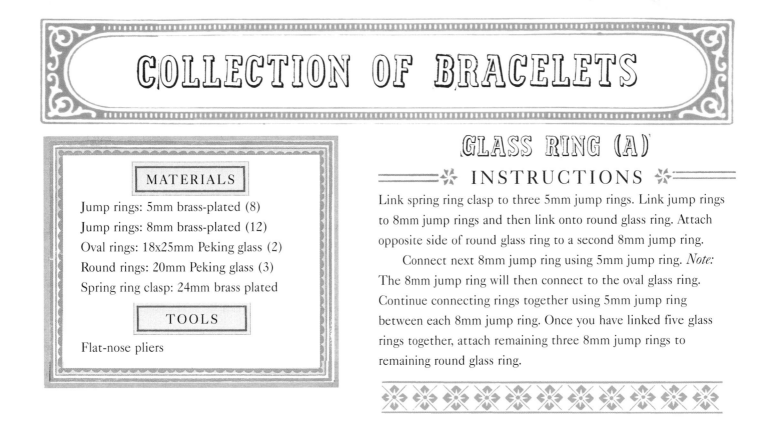

MATERIALS

Jump rings: 5mm brass-plated (8)

Jump rings: 8mm brass-plated (12)

Oval rings: 18x25mm Peking glass (2)

Round rings: 20mm Peking glass (3)

Spring ring clasp: 24mm brass plated

TOOLS

Flat-nose pliers

GLASS RING (A)

❋ INSTRUCTIONS ❋

Link spring ring clasp to three 5mm jump rings. Link jump rings to 8mm jump rings and then link onto round glass ring. Attach opposite side of round glass ring to a second 8mm jump ring.

Connect next 8mm jump ring using 5mm jump ring. *Note:* The 8mm jump ring will then connect to the oval glass ring. Continue connecting rings together using 5mm jump ring between each 8mm jump ring. Once you have linked five glass rings together, attach remaining three 8mm jump rings to remaining round glass ring.

GLASS COIN (B)

❋ INSTRUCTIONS ❋

Link glass coin beads together using twelve eye pins to make 7" strand of beads.

Glue crystal cabochons onto one side of glass coin beads; set aside to dry. Glue rose pressed-glass cabochon to flat disk; set aside to dry.

Once crystals have dried on beads, attach 8mm jump ring to end of strand. On opposite end, attach 5mm jump ring and clasp. Attach pressed-glass charm and glass leaf bead to same 5mm jump ring.

Attach charm using 5mm jump ring. Thread leaf onto head pin and create loop at end; attach to bracelet.

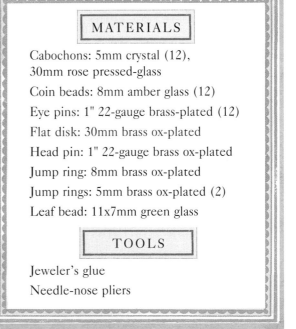

MATERIALS

Cabochons: 5mm crystal (12),
30mm rose pressed-glass

Coin beads: 8mm amber glass (12)

Eye pins: 1" 22-gauge brass-plated (12)

Flat disk: 30mm brass ox-plated

Head pin: 1" 22-gauge brass ox-plated

Jump ring: 8mm brass ox-plated

Jump rings: 5mm brass ox-plated (2)

Leaf bead: 11x7mm green glass

TOOLS

Jeweler's glue
Needle-nose pliers

MATERIALS

Cable chain: 8mm brass-ox plated (7")

Jump ring: 8mm brass-ox plated

Jump rings: 5mm brass-ox plated (14)

Pearls embedded with wire 14mm glass (15)

Sequins: 9mm (13)

Spring ring clasp: 12mm brass-ox plated

TOOLS

Needle-nose pliers

GLASS PEARL DROP (C)
❈ INSTRUCTIONS ❈

Attach spring ring clasp to one end of chain using 5mm jump ring. Attach 8mm jump ring to opposite end. Lay chain down with clasp on left side.

Attach glass pearl to each large link by opening wire loop and looping back around chain link. Attach sequins using 5mm jump rings to each of the smaller links.

SMALL LINKED (D)
❈ INSTRUCTIONS ❈

Glue each mother-of-pearl cabochon onto bezel. Glue nailhead glass on top of mother-of-pearl cabochon; set aside to dry.

Thread each eye pin with vermeil bead, glass coin, and a second vermeil bead; cut and loop closed.

Once glue on bezels has dried, link coin bead and vermeil beads to mother-of-pearl cabochons using 3mm jump rings. Continue this pattern until 7" length of links is reached. Attach 3mm and 8mm jump rings to one end and 3mm and 5mm jump rings and clasp to opposite end.

MATERIALS

Beads: 2mm vermeil (8)

Cabochons: 8mm mother-of-pearl (5)

Coin beads: 5mm cranberry glass (4)

Double ring bezels: 8x8mm brass-ox plated (5)

Eye pins: 1" 22-gauge brass-ox plated (4)

Jump ring: 5mm brass-ox plated

Jump ring: 8mm brass-ox plated

Jump rings: 3mm brass-ox plated (10)

Nailhead beads: 5mm green glass (5)

Spring ring clasp: 24mm brass-ox plated

TOOLS

Cement glue

Needle-nose pliers

Wire cutters

MATERIALS

Jump rings: 3mm brass-ox plated (25)

Round rings: green & blue 14mm glass (9)

Spring ring clasp: 12mm brass-ox plated

TOOLS

Flat-nose pliers

SMALL GLASS RING (E)
❋ INSTRUCTIONS ❋

Link spring clasp to 3mm jump ring and attach to 14mm glass ring. Connect three more 3mm jump rings to glass ring. Before closing third jump ring, connect to another glass ring. Continue connecting rings together using three 3mm jump rings. No need to add a large jump ring at the end—the clasp can connect to one of the glass rings to close bracelet.

FAVORITES

GLASS RINGS

Glass rings were manufactured in Japan from the 1920s through the 1950s. They were sewn onto clothing as trim as well as used in jewelry making.

Some time ago, I came across a large stock of these old rings—some very fine, less than 4mm thick, while others measured up to 8mm. Linked together, glass rings make great belts. Or, sewn onto clothing, they add an elegant trim.

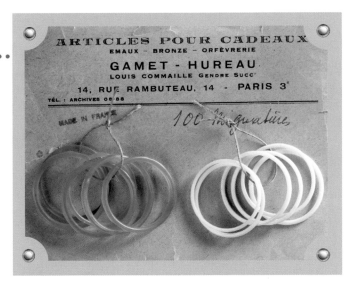

RIBBON CHARM NECKLACE

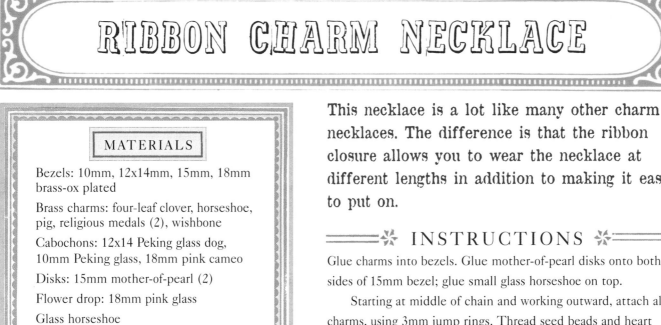

MATERIALS

Bezels: 10mm, 12x14mm, 15mm, 18mm brass-ox plated

Brass charms: four-leaf clover, horseshoe, pig, religious medals (2), wishbone

Cabochons: 12x14 Peking glass dog, 10mm Peking glass, 18mm pink cameo

Disks: 15mm mother-of-pearl (2)

Flower drop: 18mm pink glass

Glass horseshoe

Head pins: 1" brass-ox plated (2)

Heart beads: 6mm ruby glass (2)

Jump rings: 3mm brass-ox plated (11)

Jump rings: 8mm brass-ox plated (2)

Ribbon: jacquard (12")

Seed beads: 2mm gold (2)

TOOLS

Cement glue

Flat-nose pliers

Needle-nose pliers

This necklace is a lot like many other charm necklaces. The difference is that the ribbon closure allows you to wear the necklace at different lengths in addition to making it easy to put on.

❄ INSTRUCTIONS ❄

Glue charms into bezels. Glue mother-of-pearl disks onto both sides of 15mm bezel; glue small glass horseshoe on top.

Starting at middle of chain and working outward, attach all charms, using 3mm jump rings. Thread seed beads and heart beads onto head pins; cut and loop directly onto chain.

Attach 8mm jump rings to both ends of chain and thread ribbon through rings. *Note:* When wearing this necklace, slip the ribbon and chain over your head and pull the ribbon to the desired length.

DESIGN TIP

USING A RIBBON CLAMP

A small brass clamp can be added at the end of a ribbon if you want to add on a clasp. Simply fold over the clamp onto both sides of ribbon and squash close with flat-nose pliers. Ribbon clamps are available in standard ribbon widths.

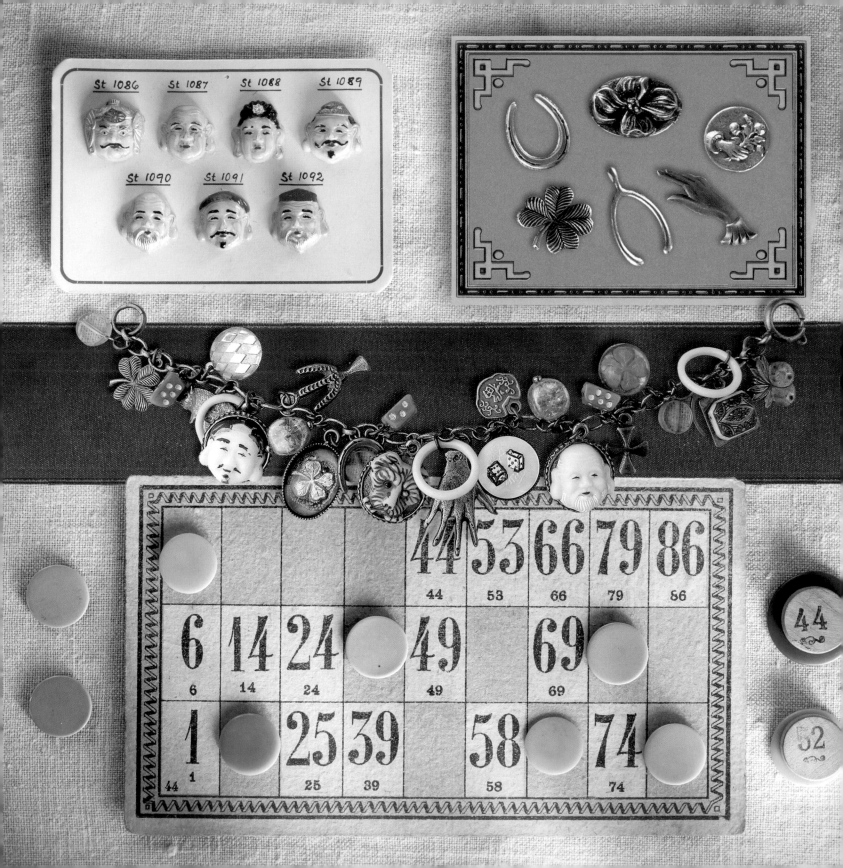

LUCKY CHARM BRACELET

MATERIALS

Bezel: 9x15mm brass-ox plated
Bezel: 14x10mm brass-ox plated
Bezels: 13mm brass-ox platcd (3)
Bezels: 18mm brass-ox plated (3)
Buddha cabochons: 18mm glass (3)
Cable chain: 8mm brass-ox plated (7½")
Carnival beads: 12mm glass (2)
Charms: brass (9)
Coin beads: 9mm amber glass (3)
Dice beads: 9x4mm pink glass (3)
Eye cabochon: 12x9mm glass
Jump ring: 9mm ox-plated
Jump rings: 5mm ox-plated (25)
Painted glass checkered cabochon: 13mm
Painted glass clover cabochon: 13mm
Painted glass clover cabochon: 14x10mm
Painted glass dice cabochon: 13mm
Round rings: 14mm green glass (3)
Seed beads: 2mm gold (4)

TOOLS

Flat-nose pliers
Jeweler's glue
Needle-nose pliers

❄ INSTRUCTIONS ❄

Glue cabochons into their respective bezels; set aside to dry. Connect clasp to one end of chain using 5mm jump ring.

Connect 9mm jump ring to opposite end of chain. Lay clasp on left side and attach charms and remaining cabochons at every large cable link using 5mm jump rings. Thread all beads onto head pins; cut and loop directly onto chain.

DESIGN TIP

ANTIQUING METAL CHARMS

To make charms appear as if they are centuries old, mix a small nugget of liver of sulphur with ½ cup of warm water. Dip the charm into this mixture. In another glass, mix 1 teaspoon of baking soda with warm water. When the charm has reached its desired color—usually 3–4 minutes—place the charm into the baking soda mixture to stop the blackening. Rinse off with warm water and let dry. A much easier way to antique metal is to allow it to soak overnight in a glass of water with a hard-boiled egg.

LA VOLIÉRE

Turn-of-the-last-century French voliéres were built to allow birds to have a large living space that would mimic their natural environment. Bird collectors would house many different species and then use their eggs and nests as natural embellishments in their own home. The colors of the aviary—turquoise blues, smoky topaz, and crystal—inspired me to design a collection of jewelry with our winged friends in mind.

Be on the lookout for old high-domed cabochons that can be used as eggs in many of the projects. If you can't find these exact cabochons, try looking for rice-shaped freshwater pearls—these too make great old-looking eggs.

This imported article of synthetic phenolic resin was manufactured by a foreign concern in no wise connected with the Bakelite Corp. and American corpor.

MADE IN CZECHOSLOVAKIA.

EGG CHARM BRACELET

MATERIALS

Bezels: 10x8mm brass-plated (8)

Bezels: 14x10mm brass-plated (16)

Bezels: 18x13mm brass-plated (14)

Bezels: 25x18mm brass-plated (4)

Cable chain: 7mm brass-plated (24")

Cabochons: 10x8mm glass (16)

Cabochons: 14x10 mm glass (32)

Cabochons: 18x13mm glass (28)

Cabochons: 25x18mm glass (8)

Cord: elastic (20")

Jump rings: 3mm brass-plated (43)

TOOLS

Flat-nose pliers

Jeweler's glue

Scissors

This is a big, very heavy charm bracelet filled with vintage glass cabochons that resemble speckled eggs. By gluing the cabochons to both sides of the bezel, we were able to make the pieces double-sided, which gives them their egg-like appearance.

❄ INSTRUCTIONS ❄

Glue glass cabochons into their respective bezels; set aside to dry. Glue matching cabochon onto opposite side of bezel. Once dry, attach egg charms onto every fourth link of chain using jump rings. Continue attaching charms until you have filled entire length of chain.

Attach ends of chain together using jump ring. Fold elastic cord in half and thread through every link of chain, cinching to fit your wrist. Tie ends of elastic together four times tightly. Add drop of jeweler's glue to secure knot. Trim excess elastic cord.

DESIGN TIP

FITTING OLD GLASS & NEW BEZELS

Vintage glass cabochons often do not fit into newly made brass bezels, so a little fudging may be required. A slightly larger bezel is usually a better choice than a smaller one. When gluing bezels, have a dish of white rice handy. Once you have glued the cabochon onto the bezel, lay it flat in the rice, which will hold the bezel in place while the cabochon dries.

SOCIETÀ VENEZIANA CONTERIE VENEZIA

oiseaux
du
paradis

FEATHER NECKLACE

MATERIALS

Beads: 4x6mm crystal matte (12)
Beads: 15x8 aqua feather glass (10)
Cable chain: 5mm gold-plated (3")
Head pin: 1" gold-plated
Jump rings: 5mm gold-plated (2)
Spring ring clasp: 9mm gold-plated
Wire: 22-gauge gold-plated (30")

TOOLS

Needle-nose pliers
Wire cutters

These projects use the wire wrap technique to make a linked necklace and earring set. Using a finer gauge wire makes it easier to wrap a loop.

❋ INSTRUCTIONS ❋

Cut wire into 2" pieces. Wire wrap loop at one end then thread on crystal bead; continue until you have eleven wire-wrapped beads.

Attach feather bead to loop at end of crystal bead and make another wire wrapped loop. Continue adding crystal then feather bead and wire wrap in between each bead until you have twenty-one wire-looped beads—or an 18" necklace. Attach clasp to one end of "chain" using 5mm jump ring; attach 3" piece of chain to opposite end using 5mm jump ring. *Note:* The extra chain will serve as the extension for a longer necklace. Attach crystal bead to head pin and attach to chain using wire loop technique.

CRYSTAL EARRINGS
❋ INSTRUCTIONS ❋

Following same technique as feather necklace, cut wire into 2" pieces. Thread on seed bead, crystal bead, and a second seed bead; wire wrap both sides. Continue to wire wrap each bead until there are four wire wrapped beads.

Connect three more beads in same manner. Finish first strand with head pin threaded with seed bead, crystal, and a second seed bead. Make wire wrapped loop and connect to other four crystal beads. *Note:* Each earring will have four strands: two with three beads, one with four, and one with five.

Connect one three-bead strand to five-bead strand after first bead. Connect all three strands to earring wire using jump ring. Repeat steps to make second earring.

MATERIALS

Beads: 4x6mm crystal matte (30)
Ear wires: gold-plated (2)
Head pins: 1" gold-plated (8)
Jump rings: 5mm gold-plated (2)
Seed beads: 2mm silver-lined aqua (60)
Wire: 22-gauge gold-plated (30")

TOOLS

Needle-nose pliers
Wire cutters

BIRD COMBS

Inspired by old millinery decorations, these hair combs are delicate, yet still have a lot to say. One is adorned with a wire nest filled with eggs and a watchful bird. You can also use colored pearls for the eggs.

MATERIALS

Beads embedded with wire: 3mm green glass (12), 6mm white stamen glass (16)

Bird: 18mm glass

Hair comb: 2" antique brass-plated

Leaves: 5x6mm blue glass (4)

Pearls: 4mm glass (3)

Wire: 22-gauge antiqued (18")

TOOLS

Jeweler's glue

Needle-nose pliers

Wire cutters

INSTRUCTIONS

To make either comb: Wrap 18" piece of wire around comb several times to secure. Form small circles on comb by weaving ends of wire in and out of "teeth."

To form nest: Start coiling 20" piece of wire and weave end in and out to hold nest together. Press down with thumb to keep bowl-shaped nest. Tuck in ends and trim extra wire.

To make branches: Twist green or white wired glass together and wrap onto comb. Glue on glass bird pearls using jeweler's glue.

NEST BROOCH

INSTRUCTIONS

To make the nest: Cut 24" piece of 20-gauge wire. Start coiling long piece of 20-gauge wire while weaving in and out of coils with shorter piece of same wire to form nest. Continue wrapping wire (the coils will get larger and larger). Press down with your thumb to keep the nest bowl-shaped.

Using 24-gauge wire, attach bar pin to back of nest by looping wire through holes on pin. Attach leaf and flowers to nest using embedded wire. Glue blue egg beads to center of nest.

MATERIALS

Bar pin: 1" brass

Eggs: 12x9mm blue glass (3)

Flowers embedded with wire: 10x10mm blue glass (3)

Leaf embedded with wire: 15x30mm pearl glass

Wire: 20-gauge gold-ox (72")

Wire: 24-gauge gold-ox (6")

TOOLS

Jeweler's glue

Needle-nose pliers

MATERIALS

Bezel: 7x10 brass-ox plated

Bezel: 10x14mm brass-ox plated

Bezels: 6x8mm brass-ox plated (3)

Cable chain: 3mm brass-ox plated (20")

Cable chain: 3mm brass-ox plated (23")

Cabochon: 10x14mm opal glass

Cabochon: 7x10mm milk glass

Cabochon: 6x8mm opal glass

Cabochons: 6x8mm speckled glass (2)

Charms: brass-ox plated (4)

Egg beads: 11x18mm teal glass (5)

Feather beads: 6x9mm white glass (20)

Figaro chain: 9mm brass-ox plated (17")

Head pins: 1" brass-ox plated (31)

Jump rings: 10mm brass-ox plated (2)

Leaves: 6x9mm blue glass (6)

Oval jump rings: 3x4mm brass-ox plated (15)

Spring ring clasp: 12mm brass-ox plated

TOOLS

Jeweler's glue

Needle-nose pliers

Wire cutters

❋ INSTRUCTIONS ❋

Glue cabochons into their respective bezels; set aside to dry.

To make first strand: Locate center link in figaro chain. Thread egg bead onto head pin, then cut and loop directly onto chain. Thread two more egg beads onto two head pins and attach to either side, approximately 1¾" apart.

To make second strand: Thread feather beads onto head pins, then cut and loop directly onto 20" cable chain ½" apart.

To make third strand: Attach 10x14mm opal charm to center of 23" piece of chain using oval jump ring. Attach three leaves, two charms, and two speckled cabochons to either side of opal using oval jump rings, leaving about ½" between each bead. Continue attaching leaves, charms, and cabochons to opposite side of chain to balance out third strand.

Attach clasp to end of all three strands using 10mm jump ring. Attach remaining 10mm jump ring to opposite ends of chain.

DESIGN TIP

EXTENDING THE LENGTH

Chain extensions are great for making chokers into longer necklaces, lending versatility to any short necklace. Simply add an extension of chain—at least 3"—to the back of the necklace using a jump ring. You can also dangle an embellishment threaded onto a head pin off the end of the chain for a decorative touch. Another way to create an extension is to link four to five 5mm jump rings together at the end of a necklace.

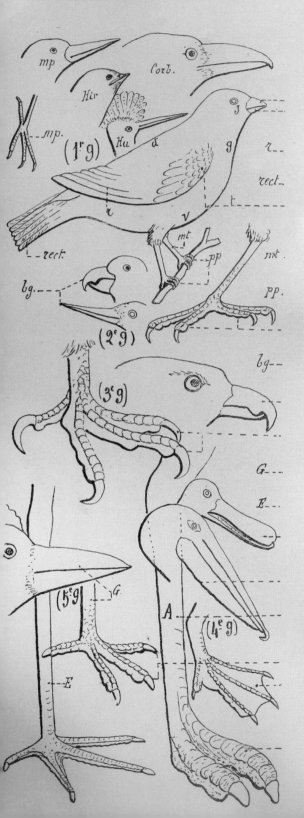

GLASS RING NECKLACE

Using my favorite glass rings and beads to match, this hand-wired necklace is elegant enough to be worn as a long necklace or wrapped around your waist as a belt.

MATERIALS

Beads: 3mm vermeil (30)
Cable chain: 9mm gold-plated oval (8")
Clasp: 9mm gold-plated
English-cut beads: 6mm aqua (15)
Jump rings: 5mm gold-plated (3)
Rings: 30mm blue glass (15)
Wire: 24-gauge gold (45")

TOOLS

Needle-nose pliers
Wire cutters

INSTRUCTIONS

Cut gold wire into fifteen 3" pieces. Onto each wire piece, thread vermeil bead, aqua bead, and a second vermeil bead; wire wrap each end around glass ring. Continue threading and wrapping onto all remaining glass rings.

Cut oval chain in half. Connect 4" piece of oval chain to last glass ring using 5mm jump ring. Connect clasp using second jump ring. On opposite end of rings, connect last piece of 4" oval chain using 5mm jump ring.

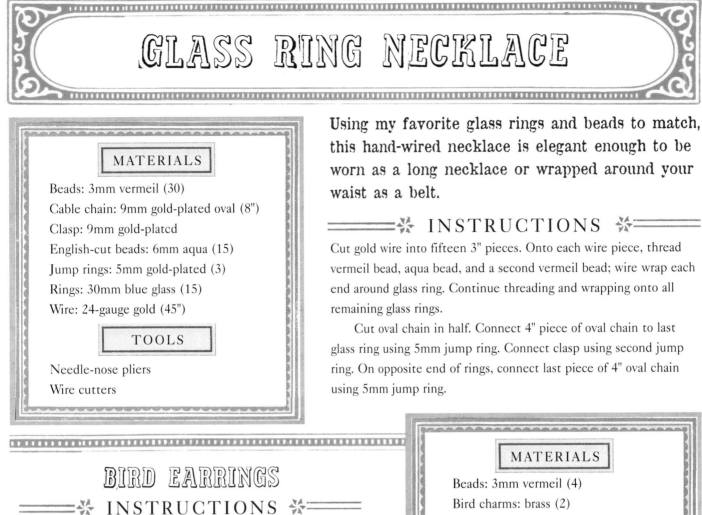

BIRD EARRINGS

INSTRUCTIONS

Cut chain in half and attach 3mm jump ring at each end. Attach bird charm to one end.

Attach 5mm jump ring to glass ring, then attach 3mm jump ring at top of chain holding bird. Thread vermeil bead, oval bead, and a second vermeil bead onto eye pin; cut and loop onto 5mm jump ring holding ring and bird on chain. Attach ear wire to opposite end of eye pin. Repeat steps to make second earring.

MATERIALS

Beads: 3mm vermeil (4)
Bird charms: brass (2)
Cable chain: 2mm gold-plated (1")
Ear wires: gold-plated (2)
Eye pins: 1" gold-plated (2)
Jump rings: 3mm gold-plated (4)
Jump rings: 5mm gold-plated (2)
Oval beads: 15x13mm aqua glass (2)
Rings: 30mm blue glass (2)

TOOLS

Needle-nose pliers
Wire cutters

LE VIGNE

> ❝ The fallen hazel-nuts,
>   Stripped late of their green sheaths,
>   The grapes, red-purple,
>   Their berries dripping with wine,
>   Pomegranates already broken,
>   And shrunken fig,
>   And quinces untouched,
>   I bring thee as offering. ❞
>
> —*Hilda Doolittle, 1886–1961*

Driving through vineyard country, you can almost see nature's entire palette—all the old purples from the grapes, the deep greens of the vines, and the blossoms that grow in between. The vineyard and orchard are wonderful sources of inspiration for a rich palette.

The idea of designing a line around a very organic element, even allowing the color of the vine and the dirt to be a part of the palette, appeals to me. Cultivating a palette based on organic, rustic colors creates versatile jewelry that can be worn through any season.

VINS DE TABLE

VIN ROUGE

le verre . . . .

le quart . . . .

la demie . . . .

VIN BLANC

le verre . . . .

le quart . . . .

la demie. . . . .

VINS FINS

bout.   demie

Côt.-du-Rhône. . . . . . .

Beaujolais . . . .

Pelure d'oignon . . . . .

Blanc . . . .

MENU MODERNE   DID. 60 – 08

DRIPPING BERRY NECKLACE

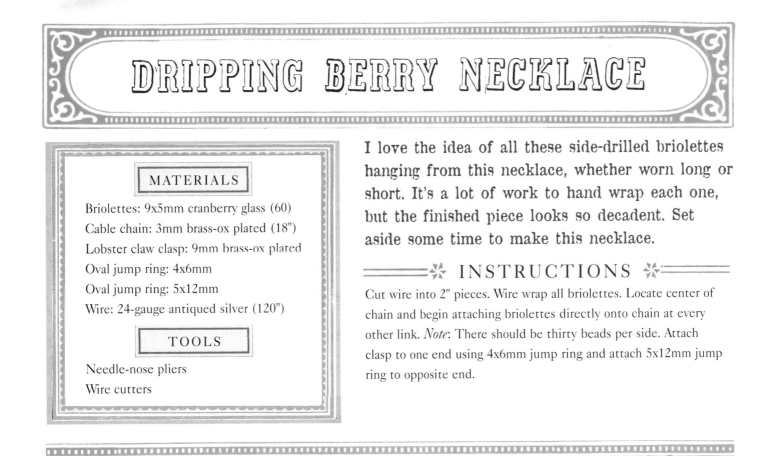

MATERIALS

Briolettes: 9x5mm cranberry glass (60)

Cable chain: 3mm brass-ox plated (18")

Lobster claw clasp: 9mm brass-ox plated

Oval jump ring: 4x6mm

Oval jump ring: 5x12mm

Wire: 24-gauge antiqued silver (120")

TOOLS

Needle-nose pliers

Wire cutters

I love the idea of all these side-drilled briolettes hanging from this necklace, whether worn long or short. It's a lot of work to hand wrap each one, but the finished piece looks so decadent. Set aside some time to make this necklace.

❊ INSTRUCTIONS ❊

Cut wire into 2" pieces. Wire wrap all briolettes. Locate center of chain and begin attaching briolettes directly onto chain at every other link. *Note*: There should be thirty beads per side. Attach clasp to one end using 4x6mm jump ring and attach 5x12mm jump ring to opposite end.

CRANBERRY DROP EARRINGS

❊ INSTRUCTIONS ❊

Glue cabochons into bezels; set aside to dry. Thread eye pin through opal bead and loop top to ear wire.

Thread a second eye pin through fuchsia bead and loop to opal bead. Loop opposite end of fuchsia eye pin onto cabochon. Repeat steps to make second earring.

MATERIALS

Bezels: 5x7mm brass-ox plated (2)

Cabochons: 5x7mm fuchsia glass (2)

Ear wires: brass-ox plated (2)

Eye pins: 1" brass-ox plated (4)

Teardrop beads: 5x7mm fuchsia glass (2)

Teardrop beads: 8x19mm opal glass (2)

TOOLS

Jeweler's glue

Needle-nose pliers

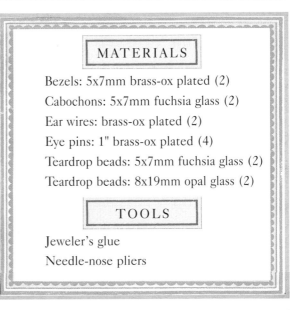

TOUJOURS ET A JAMAIS

VINE TRELLIS LARIAT

Using seed beads and glass leaves, I strung, wove, and twisted beads together then added a cluster of grapes at the bottom to create this lariat necklace.

MATERIALS

Beads: 4mm champagne glass (10)
Beads: 6mm Montana blue glass (4)
Briolettes: 5x7mm variegated blue-green glass (14)
Bugle beads: 3mm black iris glass (400)
Cable chain: 3mm gold-plated (2")
Cord: 0.45mm silk (160")
Head pins: 1" gold-plated (22)
Jump rings: 3mm gold-plated (4)
Leaves: 4x8mm matte gray glass (4)
Leaves: 7x13mm brown iris glass (7)
Leaves: 7x13mm green glass (8)
Leaves: 9x14mm green glass (9)
Seed beads: 2mm green (880)
Seed beads: 3mm brown (750)
Wire: 24-gauge gold-plated (28")

TOOLS

Jeweler's glue
Needle-nose pliers
Wire cutters

✯ INSTRUCTIONS ✯

Tie ends of three 52" lengths of silk cord onto 3mm jump ring and make a double knot. Trim short ends and add dot of glue to secure knots. While glue is still tacky, thread one cord strand with iris bugle beads, one strand with green seed beads, and one strand with brown seed beads; hide tail ends of silk cord by tucking into beads. Continue threading beads onto each strand until 2" length is reached.

Thread strand of green seed beads through small green leaf and then twist remaining two strands around green strand before threading them through leaf. Continue in this manner, threading seed beads to create eighteen 2"–3" sections, alternating each type of leaf. *Note:* Remember to constantly twist the two strands before threading them through the leaf.

When you have finished threading eighteen sections—or 48"—finish opposite end in same manner as first step by tying three strands around a second 3mm jump ring and dabbing with glue to secure knot.

Cut chain into two 1" sections and attach piece of chain to each end of strand using 3mm jump ring. Cut wire into fourteen 2" pieces. Wire wrap two briolettes directly onto every link of chain except for last link, which should have only one briolette. Thread champagne and blue glass beads onto head pins; cut and loop. Fill in links with these beads to form clusters. Attach three leaves to top of each cluster. *Note:* These leaves can be threaded with a head pin and attached directly to the jump rings to cover the knots.

CLUSTERED BRACELET

This bracelet has also been called the Cha-Cha Bracelet. It's made on an expansion bracelet, which can be embellished with beads or charms attached using head pins.

❉ INSTRUCTIONS ❉

Thread all eighty-one vermeil beads and eighty-one 7mm crystal beads including dusty pink, garnet, brown, and green glass onto head pins; cut and loop head pins. Once all beads have been looped closed, attach four beaded pins to one 3mm jump ring and connect to a loop on the expansion bracelet.

Open jump ring and add two 4mm pearls, two 2mm seed pearls, and one 7mm glass bead. Attach jump ring to loops on bracelet at every other bar until you have completely filled entire bracelet. Attach remainder of looped beads on head pins directly onto every other bar of bracelet.

CLIP-ON EARRINGS

❉ INSTRUCTIONS ❉

Thread head pins through back of earring disk and make loop on front of earring.

Thread all beads onto head pins. Thread all of the vermeil beads along with a 7mm bead. Loop three beaded pins onto each wire loop on front of earring, in a random pattern. *Note:* Each loop should have three beads attached to it, except the center loop, which should have only the 12mm cranberry bead.

When finished attaching beads, adhere rubber pads to inside back of earring using jeweler's glue.

Hope shall
brighten
days to come,
And memory
gild the
past
Moore

BLOSSOM NECKLACE

MATERIALS

Bead: 7x13mm garnet pressed-glass

Beads: 2mm vermeil (6)

Cable chain: 3mm gold-plated (42")

Cable chain: 6mm gold-plated (20")

Eye pins: 1" gold-plated (15)

Filligree beaded flower: 25mm

Firepolish beads: 4mm bronze (15)

Firepolish beads: 4mm smoky topaz (6)

Head pins: 1" gold-plated (33)

Jump rings: 5mm gold-plated (3)

Leaves: 5x7mm variegated green glass (23)

Pearls: 4mm bronze (15)

Pearls: 5mm champagne (4)

Seed beads: 2mm crystal (16)

Seed beads: 2mm grass green (8)

Spring ring clasp: 9mm gold-plated

Wire: 24-gauge gold-plated (34")

TOOLS

Needle-nose pliers

Wire cutters

Cut 20" piece of 6mm cable chain. Cut 18" piece, 12" piece, and two 6" pieces of 3mm cable chain.

Using three beads to every eye pin, follow this pattern to thread beads onto eye pins and loop them together: crystal seed, smoky topaz, crystal seed; then crystal seed, bronze pearl, crystal seed; then crystal seed, smoky topaz, crystal seed; then grass green seed, champagne pearl, grass green seed. Continue repeating this pattern until you have looped fifteen beaded pins together to create rosary chain 7½" long.

To make first strand: Attach either end of beaded links with eye pins to 12" piece of chain that was cut in half.

To make second strand: Follow this pattern to thread beads onto head pins and loop them to 18" piece of 3mm cable chain: three bronze firepolish beads then bronze pearl. Continue until you have nineteen beaded pins dangling from chain.

To make third strand: Cut 2" piece of gold wire and thread through garnet bead. Wrap around filigree flower, and then wrap small loop around back of flower and attach piece to center of 20" piece of 6mm cable chain.

To attach leaves: Using briolette technique, wrap with 2" piece of gold wire, loop leaves directly to 20" chain. Thread plum pearl onto head pin and attach to chain between every two leaves. Skip four cables and hang another two leaves and one bronze pearl. Gather three chain ends using jump ring and attach directly to clasp. Gather opposite ends of chain using jump ring and close.

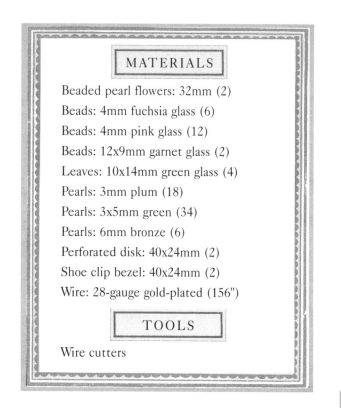

BLOSSOM SHOE CLIP-ONS
❋ INSTRUCTIONS ❋

Cut 6" piece of wire; thread seventeen green pearls onto wire. Twist ends together to form loop. Wire piece to edge of perforated disk using 12" piece of wire.

Cut 4" piece of wire and wire garnet bead to center of flower; wire to front of disk. Cut two 4" pieces of wire and wire two leaves onto disk next to flower. From under the disk, thread 24" piece of wire through hole, thread on a plum pearl, and then go back down through another hole on disk, twisting wire underneath to secure.

Continue threading wire up through another hole; add another bronze pearl and thread wire back down through a different hole. Fill in all of the perforated disk using plum pearls, bronze pearls, pink glass beads, and fuchsia glass beads. After threading on last bead, twist wire underneath disk to secure. Attach shoe clip bezel by bending prongs closed. Repeat steps to make second shoe clip.

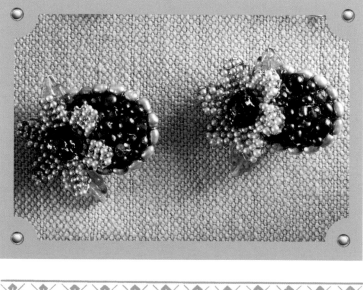

FAVORITES

FILIGREE STAMPINGS

There are wonderful old brass stampings to be found at flea markets and vintage craft stores. Using pierced stampings, you can create a piece of cagework with small beads—4mm pearls or small seed beads work great. Start with a piece of 28-gauge plated wire and begin threading the beads through the stamping.

Although the technique looks quite complicated, it is really very easy. You can sew the beads onto the filigree stamping with the wire. If you make a caged piece, you will want to work with two pieces of filigree so that one can be used on the back of the first stamping to give you a clean, finished look.

DESIGN TIP

MAKING EYE PINS

If you can't find an eye pin long enough—or short enough—consider making your own. This is easily done by cutting jewelry wire to the length you need. Make a loop at one end, thread your bead on, and then make another loop at the opposite end.

SEED BEAD BANGLES

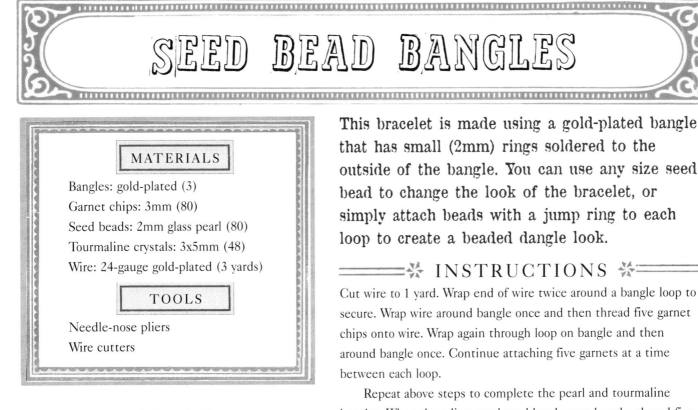

MATERIALS

Bangles: gold-plated (3)
Garnet chips: 3mm (80)
Seed beads: 2mm glass pearl (80)
Tourmaline crystals: 3x5mm (48)
Wire: 24-gauge gold-plated (3 yards)

TOOLS

Needle-nose pliers
Wire cutters

This bracelet is made using a gold-plated bangle that has small (2mm) rings soldered to the outside of the bangle. You can use any size seed bead to change the look of the bracelet, or simply attach beads with a jump ring to each loop to create a beaded dangle look.

❉ INSTRUCTIONS ❉

Cut wire to 1 yard. Wrap end of wire twice around a bangle loop to secure. Wrap wire around bangle once and then thread five garnet chips onto wire. Wrap again through loop on bangle and then around bangle once. Continue attaching five garnets at a time between each loop.

Repeat above steps to complete the pearl and tourmaline bangles. When threading pearl seed beads onto bangle, thread five onto the wire between each loop. Thread three tourmaline crystals between each loop. Once all beads are wrapped onto bracelet, wrap wire around bangle two more times.

WIRED HOOP EARRINGS

❉ INSTRUCTIONS ❉

Wrap 18" gold wire around top of hoop four times, leaving ½" on either side of top of hoop. Thread on a garnet chip and wrap wire around hoop two times before threading on next garnet chip. Continue wrapping eighteen garnet chips onto each hoop, finishing by wrapping end of hoop four times. Repeat steps to make second earring.

MATERIALS

Earring hoops: 25mm gold-plated (2)
Garnet chips: 3mm (36)
Wire: 28-gauge gold-plated (36")

TOOLS

Needle-nose pliers

LE CHATEAU

“ Rich and rare were the gems she wore,
And a bright gold ring on her hand she bore. ”

—Thomas Moore

Think of Marie Antoinette and her court of many ladies, all dressed to the nines and covered in jewels. This collection of jewelry was inspired by the deep bronzes and rich garnet colors that were worn in France when ladies were decorating themselves with layers and layers of jewels.

Although the clothing, jewels, hair ornaments, and even shoes were all ornate and heavily embellished, the jewelry translates as well today as it did when it was first made. These days, I am partial to the warm hues of gold and honey-oxidized bronze, but you can easily substitute these metals for sterling or antique silver if you prefer.

CHANDELIER NECKLACE

MATERIALS

Briolettes: 5x8mm brown iris (50)

Cable chain: 2mm gold-plated (4")

Cable chain: 4mm gold-plated (66")

Drop beads embedded with wire: 24mm topaz (7)

Eye pins: 1" gold-plated (14)

Firepolish beads: 5mm garnet (15)

Jump ring: 10mm gold-plated

Jump rings: 3mm gold-plated (11)

Jump rings: 5mm gold-plated (7)

Oval cable chain: 9mm gold-plated (4")

Spring ring clasp: 9mm gold-plated

Wire: 24-gauge gold-plated (100")

TOOLS

Needle-nose pliers

Wire cutters

❋ INSTRUCTIONS ❋

Cut wire into 2" pieces. Cut eight 3" pieces of 4mm chain. On four chain pieces, loop on eight brown iris briolettes every third link, using the briolette wrap technique.

Cut four 3¼" pieces of 4mm chain. On two of these pieces, wire loop on nine brown iris beads every third link.

To make small rectangle of beads: Thread each garnet bead onto each eye pin; cut and loop closed. Open both loops on one garnet beaded pin and loop onto two garnet beaded pins; close loops. Cut four ¼" pieces of 2mm chain. Connect one piece of chain to each corner of rectangle. Bring two ends of chain together on another looped garnet beaded pin; repeat on opposite side. Cut ½" piece of 2mm chain and connect to one garnet beaded pin. Attach 3mm jump ring to opposite side. Repeat process to create second rectangle for necklace.

Cut and loop embedded wire topaz drops, and then attach to 3mm jump rings. Cut twelve 2½" pieces of 4mm chain.

To assemble necklace: Starting at center, open 5mm jump ring and thread on one topaz drop, one 3¼" piece of chain with brown iris drops, one 3¼" piece of chain, 3mm jump ring attached to end of garnet rectangle, and two 2½" pieces of chain; close jump ring. Open a second 5mm jump ring and onto left side, thread on ends of chains in same order—brown iris drops first and 2½" piece of chain last. Onto right side of jump ring, thread on topaz drop (with 3mm jump ring attached), 3" piece of chain with brown iris drops, 3" piece of chain, and two 2½" pieces of chain; close jump ring. Repeat same process for next section. Before closing last 5mm jump ring, attach 3" of oval cable chain. Wire loop on brown iris and garnet firepolish bead to end of oval cable chain. Go back to center of necklace and open 5mm jump ring. Working from right to left, follow same pattern to create left side of necklace.

CHANDELIER EARRINGS
❊ INSTRUCTIONS ❊

Thread one vermeil bead, one garnet, and one vermeil bead onto topaz drop bead wire; cut and loop wire. Attach to center hole of brass stamping using 3mm jump ring.

Cut wire into four 2" sections. Wire wrap and loop brown iris briolettes onto either side of topaz drop. Attach brass stamping to ear wire. Repeat steps to make second earring.

DESIGN TIP

SUBSTITUTING BRIOLETTES

If you can't find side-drilled beads, or briolettes, try using a teardrop-shaped bead in a similar size. Thread a head pin through the tear drop, cut, and then loop directly onto the chain.

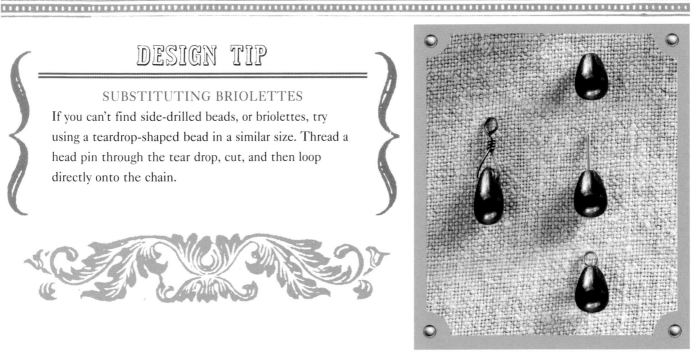

DESIGN TIP

SETTING UP YOUR WORKSPACE

Since the Chandelier Necklace project takes a little more time to make, be sure to prepare your workspace so that you have everything you need before assembling it. When beading a piece of jewelry that has many components, I like to lay everything out on a soft cloth. This is a great way to keep beads and findings from rolling all over the place. It also gives you a small workspace that can easily be cleaned up.

I prefer to cut my chain into the desired lengths beforehand so I have them ready when I begin. You may want to keep a few extra cut pieces on hand in case you decide to make the necklace longer.

GLASS-IMITATION
STONES
SQUARES
ruby

mm
SS 4x4

FIVE-STRAND PEARL BRACELET

MATERIALS

5-strand connectors: 1" antique gold (2)

5-strand spacers: 1" antique gold (2)

Bead tips: 3mm brass-ox plated (10)

Belly beads: 4x5mm fuchsia (13)

Belly beads: 4x5mm garnet (20)

Cord: 0.45mm silk (40")

Head pin: 1" brass-ox plated 22-guage

Jump rings: 3mm brass-ox plated (10)

Jump rings: 9x6mm oval brass-ox plated (6)

Pearl: 9mm aubergine glass

Pearls: 5mm champagne (17)

Pearls: 5mm plum (19)

Pearls: 10mm rose glass (5)

Seed beads: 2mm hematite (174)

Seed beads: 2mm vermeil (53)

Spring ring clasp: 12mm brass-ox plated

TOOLS

Flat-nose pliers

Jeweler's glue

Needle-nose pliers

This bracelet adds a bit of glamour to your wrist. Originally I designed this piece on elastic, which allowed me to get it on and off easily, but it did not have the same elegance as when I strung it.

❈ INSTRUCTIONS ❈

Knot end of silk cord. Add dab of glue to knot and thread on bead tip; close bead tip using flat-nose pliers.

Begin first strand by threading three hematite seed beads, vermeil seed bead, twelve hematite seed beads, vermeil seed bead, and garnet belly bead onto cord. Thread this first strand through first hole on spacer bar.

Continue first strand by stringing on garnet belly bead, vermeil seed bead, fuchsia belly bead, champagne freshwater pearl, fuchsia belly bead, vermeil seed bead, three hematite seed beads, champagne freshwater pearl, three hematite seed beads, vermeil seed bead, plum freshwater pearl, vermeil seed bead, three hematite seed beads, champagne freshwater pearl, three hematite seed beads, vermeil seed bead, fuchsia belly bead, champagne pearl, fuchsia belly bead, vermeil seed bead, and garnet belly bead. Thread through first hole on second spacer bar.

Repeat first section of strand in reverse by threading on garnet belly bead, vermeil seed bead, twelve hematite seed beads, vermeil seed bead, and three hematite seed beads. Finish first strand by threading on a second bead tip and tying knot; add dab of glue to knot and close bead tip. Knot silk cord; thread on bead tip and close.

Begin second strand by knotting end of silk cord. Add dab of glue to knot and thread on bead tip; close bead tip. Thread same hematite-vermeil-garnet belly bead pattern from first strand. Thread through second hole of spacer bar.

Continue second strand by stringing on garnet belly bead, vermeil seed bead, plum freshwater pearl, fuchsia belly bead, plum freshwater pearl, vermeil seed bead, champagne freshwater pearl, vermeil seed bead, plum freshwater pearl, fuchsia belly bead, vermeil seed bead, champagne freshwater pearl, vermeil seed bead, fuchsia belly bead, plum freshwater pearl, vermeil seed bead, champagne freshwater pearl, vermeil seed bead, plum freshwater pearl, fuchsia belly bead, plum freshwater pearl, vermeil seed bead, and garnet belly bead. Thread through second hole of second spacer and finish with knot and bead tip.

Begin third strand as first two strands. Continue third strand following spacer by stringing on garnet belly bead, vermeil seed bead, plum freshwater pearl, rose pearl, plum freshwater pearl, rose pearl, vermeil seed bead, aubergine freshwater pearl, vermeil seed bead, rose pearl, plum pearl, rose pearl, plum freshwater pearl, vermeil seed bead, and garnet belly bead.

Begin fourth strand as first three. Continue fourth strand by stringing on garnet belly bead, vermeil seed bead, plum freshwater pearl, vermeil seed bead, champagne freshwater pearl, fuchsia belly bead, champagne freshwater pearl, vermeil seed bead, plum freshwater pearl, vermeil seed bead, champagne freshwater pearl, fuchsia belly bead, champagne freshwater pearl, vermeil seed bead, plum freshwater pearl, vermeil seed bead, champagne freshwater pearl, fuchsia belly bead, champagne freshwater pearl, vermeil seed bead, plum freshwater pearl, vermeil seed bead, and garnet belly bead.

Begin fifth strand as first four. Continue fifth strand by stringing on garnet belly bead, vermeil seed bead, plum freshwater pearl, champagne freshwater pearl, plum freshwater pearl, vermeil seed bead, three hematite seed beads, champagne freshwater pearl, three hematite seed beads, vermeil seed bead, fuchsia belly bead, vermeil seed bead, three hematite seed beads, champagne freshwater pearl, three hematite seed beads, vermeil seed bead, plum freshwater pearl, champagne freshwater pearl, plum freshwater pearl, vermeil seed bead, and garnet belly bead.

Connect each bead tip to connectors using 3mm jump rings. Attach 9x6mm oval jump ring and clasp to one end of connector. Attach remaining five oval jump rings to opposite end of bracelet. Thread remaining rose pearl onto head pin along with fuchsia belly bead and vermeil seed bead; loop and attach to last jump ring.

DESIGN TIP

USING CONNECTORS & SPACER BARS

For multistrand bracelets or necklaces, try using a connector with two to five loops and a spacer bar with the same number of holes. Used together, these two findings will keep multistrands spaced and free of tangles.

100

MATERIALS

Beads: 2mm gold vermeil (8)

Belly beads: 3mm garnet (36)

Cable chain: 2mm gold-plated (9")

Ear wires: gold-plated (2)

Head pins: 1" 22-guage gold-plated (36)

Jump rings: 3mm gold-plated (2)

Seed beads: 2mm brown (10)

Seed beads: 2mm crystal (18)

TOOLS

Needle-nose pliers

Wire cutters

GARNET CASCADE EARRINGS

❋ INSTRUCTIONS ❋

Thread vermeil bead and garnet belly bead onto head pin; cut and loop. Repeat three times.

Thread crystal seed bead and garnet belly bead onto head pin; cut and loop. Repeat eight times.

Thread brown seed bead and garnet belly bead onto head pin; cut and loop. Repeat four times.

Attach ¾" piece of chain and one garnet-and-gold head pin to ear wire; close ear wire. Attach two garnet-and-gold head pins, three brown-and-garnet head pins, and seven crystal-and-garnet head pins onto ¾" piece of chain. Thread end of ¾" chain onto 3mm jump ring, along with brown-and-garnet head pin, 1" piece of chain, 1½" piece of chain, 1¼" piece of chain, and crystal-and-garnet head pin; close jump ring.

At end of each piece of chain, attach remaining garnet and vermeil beads by threading onto head pins. Repeat steps to make second earring.

DESIGN TIP

WORKING WITH SEMI-PRECIOUS STONES

Although I love working with vintage glass, there is something to be said for the colors found in real stones. It is hard to find old beads that are deep garnet or tourmaline color. Using small semi-precious stones, or chips, is a great way to incorporate these colors into your designs. Be aware that many times the holes that have been drilled into small stones are inconsistent— each one done by hand. Be sure to have plenty of extra beads on hand in case you cannot thread your wire through the hole.

SPARKLING EARRINGS

MATERIALS

Belly beads: 4mm garnet glass (22)

Cable chain: 2mm brass-ox plated (12")

Ear wires: brass-ox plated (2)

Eye pins: 1" brass-ox plated (4)

Filigree charms: brass-ox plated (2)

Firepolish beads: 4mm brown iris (2)

Flat-back rhinestones: 3mm garnet (2)

Head pins: 1" brass-ox plated (4)

Pearls: 7mm aubergine glass (2)

Seed beads: 2mm pearl (26)

Wire: 24-gauge antiqued silver (6")

TOOLS

Jeweler's glue

Needle-nose pliers

Wire cutters

Yolande
Duchesse de Polignac

HARP (A)

❈ INSTRUCTIONS ❈

Cut wire into two 3" pieces. Cut 1¾" piece of chain. Loop one end of wire, and then attach chain before closing. Thread on four garnet belly beads and four pearl seed beads, alternating each bead.

Cut 1¼" piece of chain and thread onto wire. Thread on one garnet belly bead and one seed bead.

Cut ¼" of chain and thread onto wire. Thread on one seed bead and one garnet belly bead. Cut and thread on another 1¼" piece of chain. Thread on four seed beads and four garnet belly beads, alternating each bead; cut and loop wire. Thread on another ¾" piece of chain before closing; bend wire into rounded arc. *Note:* You can use a small bobbin to make this shape.

Thread brown iris bead onto head pin; cut and loop, then attach to ¼" piece of chain hanging from center. Thread seed bead onto eye pin; cut and loop, connecting two longer pieces of chain. Open opposite end of eye pin and hang filigree charm. Thread aubergine glass pearl and pearl seed bead onto head pin; cut and loop onto ½" piece of chain.

Thread a second eye pin with garnet belly bead and pearl seed bead; cut and loop, then attach onto ear wire. Open opposite end of eye pin and thread on ¾" length of chain attached to arc (chain with aubergine pearl and then other end of chain attached to arc); close loop. Glue garnet rhinestone to filigree; let dry. Repeat steps to make second earring.

MATERIALS

Cable chain: 3mm brass-ox plated (5")

Ear wires: brass-ox plated (2)

Eye pins: 1" gold-plated (2)

Freshwater pearls: 5x7mm champagne (10)

Jump rings: 3mm gold-plated (68)

Seed beads: 2mm bronze (20)

Sequins 6mm gold (62)

Wire: 24-gauge gold-plated (4")

TOOLS

Needle-nose pliers

Wire cutters

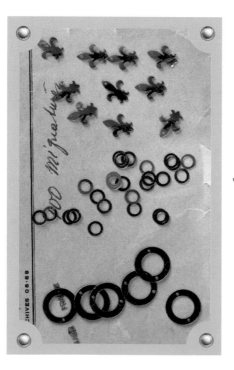

GOLD SEQUIN (B)

❖ INSTRUCTIONS ❖

Using 3mm jump rings, connect following strands of sequins: Two strands of four sequins, two strands of seven sequins, and one strand of nine sequins. *Note:* Be sure to add a jump ring to the end of each strand; this will be the end you connect onto the earring.

Cut 3mm chain into two 1" sections and one ½" section. Cut 4" piece of wire in half and, using 2" piece, form small arc by bending both ends down. Make loop on one end with needle-nose pliers. Before closing loop add on one of four-sequin strands and 1" piece of chain; close loop.

Thread seed bead and then pearl onto wire, then another seed bead and one of the seven-sequin strands, then another seed bead, pearl, seed bead, nine-sequin strand, and 2" piece of chain. Continue this pattern down rest of wire arc: seed bead, pearl, seed bead, seven-sequin strand, seed bead, pearl, and seed bead. Loop end of wire with needle-nose pliers. *Note:* Be sure to loop on four-sequin strand and 1" piece of chain before closing loop.

Thread seed bead, pearl, and seed bead onto eye pin and before closing loop, pick up all three strands of chain hanging from arc. Be sure to connect them in order—1" piece, 2" piece, and then 1" piece; close loop. Open other end of eye pin and connect to ear wire. Repeat steps to make second earring.

FAVORITES

VINTAGE SEQUINS

Using sequins on earrings, allows you to add more sparkle without worrying about a piece that is too heavy.

Sequins add a great sparkle to vintage-inspired jewelry. Look for old sequins at notion or sewing shops; they are usually sold by the thousands. Many sequins from the 1920s were made out of celluloid. Be careful not to get these wet, as they will eventually melt.

MATERIALS

Ball castings: brass-ox plated (2)

Crystal chatons: ruby with gold foil-backed (24)

Ear wires: gold-plated (2)

Eye pins: 1" gold-plated (8)

Nailhead beads: 5mm ruby glass (8)

TOOLS

Jeweler's glue

Needle-nose pliers

CRYSTAL BALL (C)

✳ INSTRUCTIONS ✳

Glue chatons into casting; set aside to dry. Using eye pins, link four nailhead beads together. Attach end of bead strand to loop on ball casting and other end of bead link to ear wire. Repeat steps to make second earring.

DESIGN TIP

WORKING WITH CHATONS

Chatons are pointed-back rhinestones that are foil-backed to give them sparkle. These stones can easily be set into metal settings with prongs or into cast settings with pre-set cavities. Pavé is a method of setting small crystals in a piece of jewelry to cover the entire surface—as if the metal appears to be pavéd with gemstones.

105

CHARM NECKLACE

MATERIALS

Bezel: 15mm 9x6 brass-ox plated
Cabochon: 9x9mm carnelian glass
Cabochon: 15mm carnelian glass with silver
Cabochon: 15x40mm carnelian glass
Charms: brass-ox plated (2)
Clasp: 30mm gold-plated
Drawn cable chain: 5mm gold-plated (38")
Flowers embedded with wire: 10mm garnet glass (2)
Head pins: 1" gold-plated (79)
Jump rings: 3mm gold-plated (16)
Nailhead beads: 4mm bronze (56)
Ring: 14x10mm carnelian glass
Ring: 25x14mm carnelian glass

TOOLS

Flat-nose pliers
Jeweler's glue
Needle-nose pliers

This necklace was designed to be worn in the front or back. Worn in layers, its a charm necklace, and worn with the charms in back, it's a delicate beaded chain.

INSTRUCTIONS

Glue cabochons to respective bezels and set aside to dry. Attach clasp to either end of chain using a 3mm jump ring on each end. Thread head pin through each of the bronze nailhead glass beads, cut and loop directly to the chain, beginning at the clasp and working downward. Once you have attached twenty-eight nailhead beads to each side, begin attaching the larger charms. In between each charm, loop on a cluster of pearl and garnet beads using a head pin. Attach largest pendant to center of chain.

FAVORITES

NAILHEAD GLASS

Nailheads are flat-backed glass beads with one or two holes parallel to the flat surface. Nailhead beads come in all sorts of colors, finishes, and shapes. Also called "sew-ons," they were made mostly for the French couture houses in the Victorian and Edwardian eras, hand sewn onto women's garments, trims, and accessories. Some of the bigger and brightly colored ones are from the early to mid-20th century.

WILL'S CIGARETTES.

CENTIPEDES.

WILL'S CIGARETTES.

MEALY BUG (FEMALE).

LE JARDIN

> " I perhaps owe having become a
> painter to flowers. "
>
> —*Claude Monet*

Ever since seeing Monet's garden in Giverny—the flowers, color, and light—I have been obsessed with collecting all sorts of glass flowers, leaves, and stamens. Many of the old glass flowers and leaves in my collection are from Venice.

The Venetians were the first Europeans to master the art of glass-making. The techniques they originated were so highly guarded that the glass blowers all had to live on the island of Murano. Eventually techniques leaked out and more European countries began to copy the delicate flowers and leaves that were so highly prized. Although there are wonderful reproduction glass flowers and leaves in a great variety of colors, finding old botanical shapes embedded with wire is a real treat.

109

Pure
Honey
Produced and Packed by
ANTON MASEK
Route 1
Mitchell, Iowa

WILLS'S CIGARETTES.

WASP LARVA &
SECTION OF NEST.

FOUR-STRAND FLORAL NECKLACE

MATERIALS

Barrel beads: 5x7mm cranberry glass (8)

Bell flower: 10x12mm glass

Cable chain: 3mm brass-ox plated (20")

Cable chain: 4mm brass-ox plated (22")

Drawn cable chain: 3mm brass-ox plated (16")

Drawn cable chain: 3mm brass-ox plated (18")

English-cut beads: 4mm pink (16)

Flower beads: 6mm glass (10)

Flower beads: 16mm glass (4)

Flower bud embedded with wire: 12x18mm molded glass

Head pins: 1" brass-ox plated (38)

Jump ring: 3mm brass-ox plated

Jump rings: 8mm brass-ox plated (3)

Spring ring clasp: 12mm brass-ox plated

TOOLS

Needle-nose pliers

Wire cutters

Dig out all of your flower and leaf beads for this project. You can either choose to stay in one color palette as I have, or mix it up and make your floral necklace multi-colored.

❋ INSTRUCTIONS ❋

To make first strand: Thread 6mm glass flowers onto head pins; cut and loop directly onto 16" chain, starting in the center and skipping every two links.

To make second strand: Loop glass bud to center of 18" chain. Thread and loop 4mm English-cut beads onto head pins and connect directly onto chain, placing six on each side of the glass flower bead.

To make third strand: Thread six cranberry barrel beads onto head pins; cut and loop directly onto 20" piece of chain, beginning in center and skipping ten links between each bead.

To make fourth strand: Thread remaining flower and cranberry beads onto head pins; cut and loop directly onto 22" piece of chain, skipping every two links.

Thread 4mm English-cut bead onto head pin then thread through center hole of bell glass flower for stamen; cut and loop onto chain. Gather four chain ends onto 3mm jump ring and attach to clasp. On opposite ends, gather four chains with 8mm jump ring, and then attach two more jump rings to make extension.

DESIGN TIP

MAKING HEAD PINS

To make your own head pins, cut 2" piece of 20- or 22-gauge wire and simply hit the end with a hammer to flatten it. If the flattened head is too thin for your larger beads, try threading a small seed bead on first.

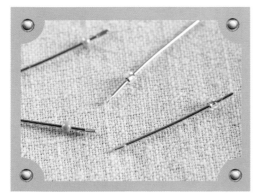

WILL'S CIGARETTES.

GRAND PRIX
ET MEMBRE DU JURY
AUX EXPOSITIONS INTERNATIONALES

EYEGLASS RING CHAIN

MATERIALS

Eyeglass connectors (2)

Flowers embedded with wire: 20mm yellow glass (4)

Head pins: 1" brass-ox plated (12)

Jump rings: 3mm brass-plated (8)

Jump rings: 9x6mm oval brass-ox plated (32)

Leaves: 5x7mm green glass (6)

Leaves: 9x12mm green glass (6)

Lobster claw: 6x12mm brass-ox plated (2)

Rings: 10x20mm oval green glass (31)

TOOLS

Needle-nose pliers

Wire cutters

This chain can also be worn as a necklace by removing the two eyeglass connectors and connecting the clasps together.

❋ INSTRUCTIONS ❋

Connect all glass rings using oval jump rings. Finish with oval jump ring at each end.

Thread one glass leaf onto each head pin; cut and loop close. Cut and loop wires on glass flowers. Connect to oval jump rings on necklace using 3mm jump rings.

Cluster flowers and leaves onto last 6" of each end of chain. Connect lobster claw to jump rings at end of strand. Connect oval jump rings to each eyeglass connector.

FLOWER RING EARRINGS

❋ INSTRUCTIONS ❋

Cut two 1½" pieces of chain; cut and loop three flowers onto chain starting with first cable and attaching at every third cable. Thread glass leaf onto each of two head pins; cut and loop directly onto chain on either side of last attached flower.

Attach 5mm jump ring to cable directly next to last attached leaf. Attach this jump ring to glass ring. Open a second 5mm jump ring and attach to top of glass ring and then to ear wire. Repeat steps to make second earring.

MATERIALS

Cable chain: 4mm brass-ox plated (6")

Ear wires: brass-ox plated (2)

Flowers embedded with wire: 20mm yellow glass (6)

Head pins: 1" brass-ox plated (4)

Jump rings: 5mm brass-ox plated (4)

Leaves: 5x7mm green glass (4)

Rings: 10x20mm oval green glass (2)

TOOLS

Needle-nose pliers

Wire cutters

VERVEINE
hybride variée
VERBENA HYBRIDA VAR.
Annuelle, vivace en serre — Verbénacées   85
Semer sur couche en mars-avril, *repiquer* sur couche
ou en petits pots, *mettre* en place en mai. On peut *semer*
également en automne et *hiverner* sous châssis
Haut 30 à 40 cent   *Fl* de juillet en octobre

MADE
IN
FRANCE

MILLINERY CORSAGE

MATERIALS

Cord: ivory silk (3")

Crystal button: 25mm

French sequins:10x15mm
aurora borealis (12)

Millinery flowers: silk magenta (9)

Picot ribbon: 1½", green (16")

Seed beads: 3mm crystal (24)

Thread

Velvet pressed leaves (3)

TOOLS

Fabric scissors

Thin needle

Who says corsages are just for the prom? Here's an idea that will make you want to start wearing flowers all year long.

❀ INSTRUCTIONS ❀

Cut ribbon into two 8" pieces. Thread needle and sew flowers and leaves together, creating bouquet. Sew bouquet to center of one piece of ribbon. Sew sequins and seed beads onto either side of flowers and leaves.

Fold silk cord in half and sew ends together, creating 1" loop with ¼" tail. Fold under ½" on both pieces of ribbon and sew ribbon pieces together around edges. Enclose silk cord at one end between the two layers of ribbon with a small stitch. Pleat ends 1"–2" wide. Sew button onto opposite end of corsage.

· · · · · · · · · FAVORITES · · · · · · · · ·

OLD MILLINERY

If you have a collection of old silk flowers or velvet pressed leaves, consider using them to make an accessory. Be sure to steam flowers or leaves to take the kinks out first. To do this, fill a tea kettle with water and boil until it whistles. Turn off the flame and hold the flower or leaves over the opening. The steam will gently take out any wrinkles and the silk will drape better.

LEAF & PETAL EARRINGS

MATERIALS

Cable chain: 3mm brass-ox plated (2")

Ear wires: brass-ox plated (2)

English-cut beads: 4mm pink (14)

Head pins: 1" brass-ox plated (14)

Jump rings: 3mm brass-ox plated (14)

Leaf stampings with loop:
5x10mm raw brass (14)

TOOLS

Needle-nose pliers

Wire cutters

LEAF & BERRIES (A)
❋ INSTRUCTIONS ❋

Cut chain into two 1" pieces. Thread English-cut beads onto head pins; cut and loop onto every third link on chain.

Attach brass leaf stampings to links next to bead on chain using 3mm jump rings. Attach ear wire loop to end of chain. Repeat steps to make second earring.

········· FAVORITES ·········
ENGLISH CUT BEADS

English cut beads are actually not cut at all, but rather crudely molded rounded beads with large irregular facets and mold marks. These beads have not been fire-polished so they tend to be more primitive and old.

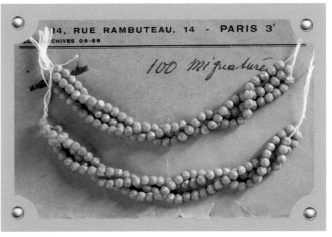

MATERIALS

Blossom stampings: 16mm raw brass (2)

Calla lily stampings: 25x10mm raw brass (2)

English-cut beads: 4mm pink (4)

Eye pins: 1" brass-ox plated (2)

Flat-front earring finding with loop: brass-ox plated (2)

Head pins: 1" brass-ox plated (2)

TOOLS

Jeweler's glue

Needle-nose pliers

Wire cutters

BLOSSOM & CALLA LILY (B)

❈ INSTRUCTIONS ❈

Glue brass flower stamping to front of earring finding. Thread English-cut bead onto eye pin and thread through brass bud bead. Attach to loop at bottom of earring.

Thread second English-cut bead onto head pin and loop through bottom of first pink bead within brass calla lily. Repeat steps to make second earring.

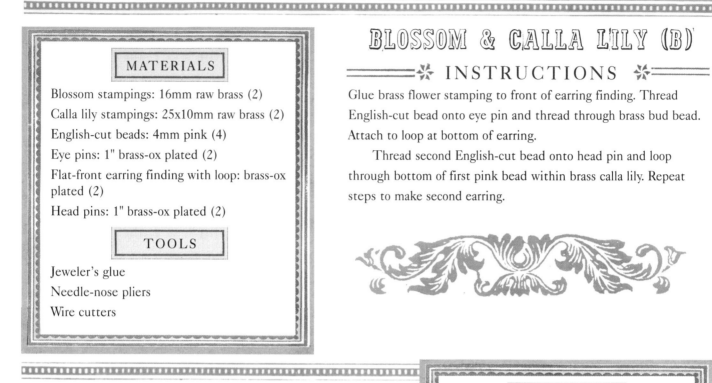

POSY CLUSTER (C)

❈ INSTRUCTIONS ❈

Glue brass flower to front of earring finding. Loop two brass leaf stampings onto 5mm jump ring and attach to loop at bottom of earring. Thread coral nailhead bead onto head pin; cut and loop onto leaf hanging at right.

Thread each English-cut bead onto separate head pin; cut and loop closed. Gather three of the English-cut beaded pins onto 3mm jump ring; attach to left side of 5mm jump ring. Gather remaining three English-cut beaded pins onto a second 3mm jump ring and attach to bottom loop of earring. Repeat steps to make second earring.

MATERIALS

English-cut beads: 4mm pink (6)

Flat-front earring findings with loop: brass-ox plated (2)

Flower stampings: 12mm raw brass (2)

Head pins: 1" brass-ox plated (14)

Jump rings: 3mm brass-ox plated (4)

Jump rings: 5mm brass-ox plated (2)

Leaf stampings with loop: 14x10mm raw brass (4)

Nailhead beads: 8mm coral glass (2)

TOOLS

Jeweler's glue

Needle-nose pliers

Wire cutters

IRIS FLORET (D)

❊ INSTRUCTIONS ❊

Glue brass iris flower stamping to front of earring finding. Thread nailhead glass bead onto eye pin and attach to loop at bottom of earring finding. Thread vermeil bead and second nailhead bead onto head pin and loop onto first nailhead bead. Repeat steps to make second earring.

MATERIALS

Beads: 3mm vermeil (2)

Eye pins: 1" brass-ox plated (2)

Flat-front earring finding with loop: brass-ox plated (2)

Head pins: 1" brass-ox plated (2)

Iris flower stampings: 25x15mm raw brass (2)

Nailhead beads: 8mm coral glass (4)

TOOLS

Jeweler's glue

Needle-nose pliers

DESIGN TIP

RAW STAMPINGS

"Raw" means just that—raw stampings that are stamped from brass sheets on greasy punch presses. These stampings are then rinsed by being passed through a dusting of dry sawdust. If you are gluing raw brass pieces to a finding, be sure to wash first with warm, soapy water, rinse, and dry thoroughly. A quick cleaning with cotton and alcohol also work well to remove any thin coats of oil before gluing.

Pour toujours et à jamais

MILLEFLEUR CHARM BRACELET

MATERIALS

Bezels: 9x11mm brass-ox plated (3)

Cable chain: 9mm brass-ox plated (7½")

Cabochon: 9x11mm opal glass (3)

Flowers: 17mm amethyst glass (2)

Flowers: 17mm cranberry glass (3)

Flowers: 17mm green glass (3)

Flowers: 17mm pink glass (3)

Head pins: 1" brass-ox plated (17)

Jump ring: 8mm brass-ox plated

Jump rings: 5mm brass-ox plated (15)

Ladybugs: 4x7mm pink glass (6)

Leaves: 5x7mm green glass (11)

Spring ring clasp: 12mm brass-ox plated

Stamens embedded with wire:
4mm milk glass (11)

TOOLS

Jeweler's glue

Needle-nose pliers

A collection of reproduction glass flowers and leaves inspired this charm bracelet. Adding in a few old opal charms gives the charm bracelet a vintage look.

❈ INSTRUCTIONS ❈

Glue opal cabochons into bezels; set aside to dry. Attach clasp to one end of chain using 5mm jump ring. Attach 8mm jump ring to opposite end of chain. *Note:* Keep the clasp on the left side while you are attaching beads so your design will face forward.

Thread milk glass stamens through all glass flowers, wrapping wire into loop at back of flower. Attach flowers to chain using 5mm jump rings, beginning at first link and attaching at every other link.

Thread leaves onto head pins; cut and loop onto opposite side of each link that has flower attached. Thread ladybugs onto head pin; cut and loop onto chain at every fourth link. Attach a brass bezel at either end and in center of bracelet using 5mm jump rings.

DESIGN TIP

GLASS STAMENS

Most pressed glass flowers will hang better off of a piece of jewelry with a beaded stamen threaded through the center. A center stamen can be made with either an embedded wire bead or by threading a head pin through a round bead and the flower and then looping directly onto the jewelry.

Iconographie de la Flore française.

MADE IN JA

FRANCE POSTES

RF 2 FR

LATHYRUS VERNUS Wimm – GESSE PRINTANIÈRE.

PEARL LATTICE BRACELET

MATERIALS

Bell flower: 10x12mm pink glass
Cable chain: 2mm gold-plated (2")
Eye pins: 2" gold-plated (54)
Head pins: 1" gold-plated (2)
Jump ring: 5mm gold-plated
Jump rings: 3mm gold-plated (16)
Leaf: 10x14mm pink glass
Pearls: 2mm glass (576)
Spring ring clasp: 9mm gold-plated

TOOLS

Needle-nose pliers
Wire cutters

❋ INSTRUCTIONS ❋

Thread twelve pearls onto eye pins; cut and loop. Repeat six times to make seven pearl bars. On a second eye pin, alternate threading a pearl bar and a pearl until you have seven pearl bars and six pearls on the eye pin.

Make six sections and then link them together using 3mm jump rings. Cut chain into four ½" pieces and attach to ends of bracelet using 3mm jump rings. Attach clasp to one end using 3mm jump ring and attach 5mm jump ring to opposite end. Thread bell glass flower onto head pin; cut and loop onto 5mm jump ring at end of bracelet. Thread glass leaf onto head pin; cut and loop next to flower bead.

PEARL EARRINGS

❋ INSTRUCTIONS ❋

Cut two 5" pieces of wire. In center of each piece of wire, make loop by crossing ends over each other. On first piece of wire, thread fourteen small pearls on either side of center loop; cut and loop ends. On second piece of wire, thread fifteen small pearls on either side of loop; cut and loop. Bend each piece of wire into a circle using your fingers. Cut 3" piece of wire; loop one end. Thread 2mm pearl and center loop of wire holding the thirty pearls onto 3" wire. Thread center loop holding the twenty-eight pearls onto 3" wire. Thread three vermeil beads, pink bell flower bead, and three vermeil beads onto 3" wire. Thread end of twenty-eight-pearl wire piece, end of thirty-pearl piece, large pearl, and one vermeil bead onto 3" wire. Thread pink leaf onto head pin and cut and loop onto bottom of earring. Using 3mm jump ring, connect loop at top onto ear wire. Repeat steps to make second earring.

MATERIALS

Beads: 3mm vermeil (12)
Bell flowers: 10x12mm pink glass (2)
Ear wires: gold-plated (2)
Head pins: 1" gold-plated (2)
Jump rings: 3mm gold-plated (2)
Leaves: 10x14mm pink glass (2)
Pearls: 2mm glass (116); 8mm glass (2)
Wire: 24-gauge gold-plated (36")

TOOLS

Needle-nose pliers
Wire cutters

SOUVENEZ-VOUS DANS VOS PRIÈRES
DE

Marguerite-Marie MOREL

PIEUSEMENT DÉCÉDÉE LE 19 JANVIER 1935

A L'AGE DE 19 ANS

C'était une âme intègre, droite, craignant Dieu et éloignée du mal.
(Job, I, 1.)

Sa mort a laissé dans nos cœurs une plaie profonde. Nous vous avions supplié, Seigneur, de prolonger ses jours. Vous lui avez donné le repos éternel, que votre Nom soit béni.
(Saint Ambroise.)

Consolez-vous donc, vous qui m'êtes si chers, car, si j'abandonne la vie dans l'âge ou tout sourit, c'est pour le royaume des Cieux. (Sainte Catherine de Sienne.)

Miséricordieux Jésus, donnez-lui le repos éternel !
(7 ans, 7 quar. d'ind.)

PHOTOGRAPHIE
DE LA
PORTE St-MARTIN

Louis

29. Bd St-M
PARI

LA CIMETIÈRE

I tend to visit a lot of churchyards in France because many of the churches I want to get into are locked during non-service hours. I am interested in the colors of a churchyard covered in fog, the stark, gray lines of the clothing worn in a convent, and the collections stored in the pockets of these cloistered individuals. Women leading these quiet lives at the turn of the last century took an active interest in the art industry. Handwork such as sewing, embroidery, and beading rosaries were all part of daily life.

In this chapter I try to imagine what was made out of the old mother-of-pearl disks, glass pearls, and crystal buttons that distinguish this time period and place.

MOTHER-OF-PEARL NECKLACE

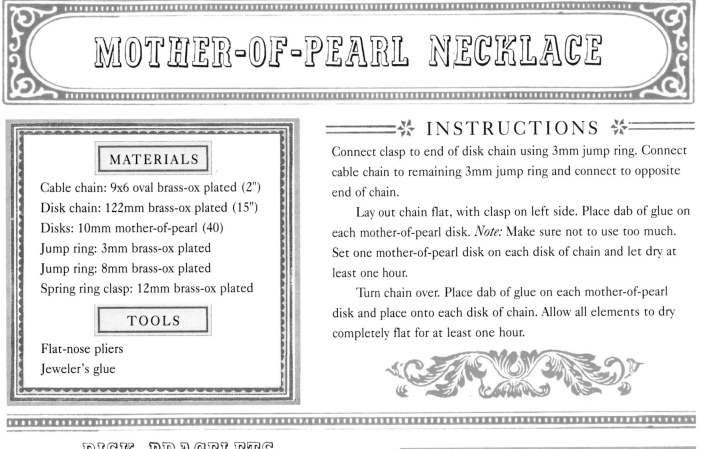

MATERIALS

Cable chain: 9x6 oval brass-ox plated (2")

Disk chain: 122mm brass-ox plated (15")

Disks: 10mm mother-of-pearl (40)

Jump ring: 3mm brass-ox plated

Jump ring: 8mm brass-ox plated

Spring ring clasp: 12mm brass-ox plated

TOOLS

Flat-nose pliers

Jeweler's glue

❈ INSTRUCTIONS ❈

Connect clasp to end of disk chain using 3mm jump ring. Connect cable chain to remaining 3mm jump ring and connect to opposite end of chain.

Lay out chain flat, with clasp on left side. Place dab of glue on each mother-of-pearl disk. *Note:* Make sure not to use too much. Set one mother-of-pearl disk on each disk of chain and let dry at least one hour.

Turn chain over. Place dab of glue on each mother-of-pearl disk and place onto each disk of chain. Allow all elements to dry completely flat for at least one hour.

DISK BRACELETS

❈ INSTRUCTIONS ❈

Connect clasp to end of chain using 3mm jump ring. Connect 8mm jump ring at opposite end.

Lay out chain flat, with clasp on left side. Place dab of glue on each mother-of-pearl disk. *Note:* Make sure not to use too much. Set one mother-of-pearl disk on each disk of chain and let dry at least one hour.

Turn chain over. Place dab of glue on each mother-of-pearl disk and place onto each disk of chain. Allow all elements to dry completely flat for at least one hour.

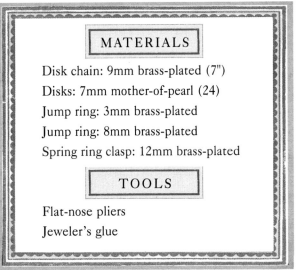

MATERIALS

Disk chain: 9mm brass-plated (7")

Disks: 7mm mother-of-pearl (24)

Jump ring: 3mm brass-plated

Jump ring: 8mm brass-plated

Spring ring clasp: 12mm brass-plated

TOOLS

Flat-nose pliers

Jeweler's glue

TEN-STRAND BRACELET

MATERIALS

5-ring connector: 22mm brass-ox plated (2)
Bugle beads: 2x5mm silver glass (165)
Cable chain: 6mm brass-ox plated (1")
Eye pins: 1" brass-ox plated (80)
Head pins: 1" brass-ox plated (6)
Jump rings: 3mm brass-ox plated (11)
Jump rings: 5mm brass-ox plated (2)
Spring ring clasp: 12mm brass-ox plated

TOOLS

Needle-nose pliers
Wire cutters

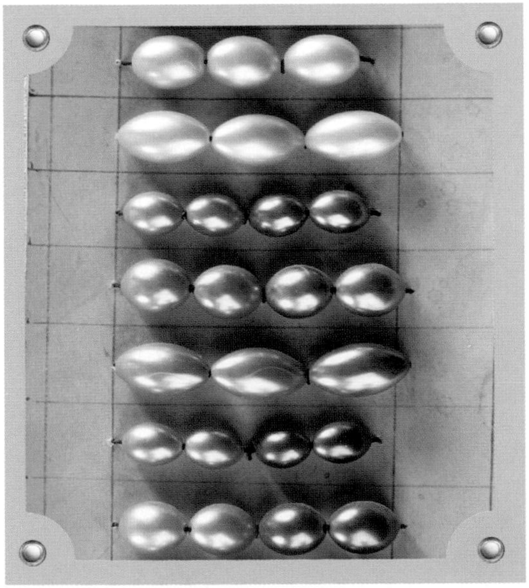

This bracelet uses two five-ring connectors which allow the strands of beads to remain close to each other without becoming entangled.

INSTRUCTIONS

Thread two bugle beads onto each eye pin. Loop eight eye pins together to form one strand, making ten strands total.

Attach 3mm jump ring to two strands and then attach to bracelet connector. Repeat on opposite end of strand.

Connect chain to one end of connector using 5mm jump ring. Thread head pins with bugle beads; cut and loop. Gather all five head pins onto 3mm jump ring; connect to end of chain. Attach clasp to opposite end of bracelet using 5mm jump ring.

DESIGN TIP

WORKING WITH OLD BEADS

Vintage beads can be wonderful to work with, but they do pose a bit of a challenge when making jewelry.

Before you begin designing your jewelry piece, gently clean glass beads by either spraying them with warm water and gently wiping with a soft cloth or dipping them in a bath of warm, sudsy water and rinsing them off. After you have cleaned the beads, lay them out and take a good look to determine if they are strong enough to last on a piece of jewelry. Many old beads have jagged edges and can fray the cord you use to string them onto, or they are too brittle to hold up under pressure when they are wire looped.

CRYSTAL BUTTON NECKLACE

MATERIALS

Crystal buttons: 9mm (60)
Disk chain: 9mm brass-plated (16")
Jump ring: 3mm brass-plated
Jump ring: 8mm brass-plated
Spring ring clasp: 30mm brass-plated

TOOLS

Flat-nose pliers
Jeweler's glue

This is another great project for beginning beaders, with only gluing involved. You can use a mixture of buttons you have collected, or buy an old button card and snip the buttons off.

❋ INSTRUCTIONS ❋

Connect clasp to end of chain using 3mm jump ring. Connect 8mm jump ring at opposite end of chain.

Lay out chain flat, with clasp on left side, and place dab of glue on each disk. *Note:* Make sure not to use too much, as you don't want the surface to overflow with glue. Set one button on each disk and let dry at least one hour.

Turn chain over. Place dab of glue on each disk and set button onto each disk; allow all elements to dry completely flat.

FAVORITES

VINTAGE BUTTONS

I first started collecting buttons when my mom brought home my grandmother's button collection. My brother, mom, and I sat and sorted through the tin full of early bakelite, celluloid, mother-of-pearl, glass, and metal buttons. We strung each grouping by similar color or design onto individual hanks and marveled at the diversity of each one.

Today I am still fascinated with old buttons and buy them whenever I can. I keep my eyes peeled for boxes of mother-of-pearl buttons on their original cards, or hanks of gold foil-backed crystal buttons. Look for buttons at estate sales, thrift shops, or flea markets.

FACTURE.   Montauban, le 18 X^{bre} 1821

Doit M^d *Sedug negt a villefranche D'aveyron*

à nous *Soleville et Comp.*, f. 88   pour notre envoi suivant

SAVOIR:

PRIX c...
SAUF I...

CAFÉ fi...

CASSON...
1.er Blan...
2.e Blan...
Blonde...
Rousse...

Eau-de-...
magna...
Girofle...

HUILE...
Surfine a...
Mi-fine...
Mangeab...
Commun...
De Noix...
De Lin...
A quinq...

Indigo fi...
Poivre en...
Riz du Pi...
Riz Caroll...
Savon ble...
Sucre en p...

N° 203 M.   COLOR
1.36 La pièce
PARIS   MADE IN FRANCE

BEADED CUFF

MATERIALS

Beads: 4mm mercury glass (4)

Bugle beads: 2x5mm silver glass (44)

Cord: mauve silk (4½")

Crosses: 10x8mm rhinestone (16)

Crystal buttons: 6mm (3)

Flower buttons: 9mm glass hematite (17)

Nailhead beads: 6mm glass hematite (32)

Nailhead flowers: 8mm black
pressed-glass (12)

Ribbon: 2"-wide mauve (8")

Seed beads: 3mm crystal (68)

Silk cord: 4½" mauve

Thread: mauve

Ultra suede: 2"-wide gray (7")

TOOLS

Beading needle

Fabric scissors

Fine needle

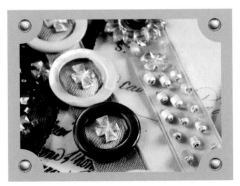

Another beautiful way to display your collection of vintage buttons and bits is to sew them onto a piece of silk ribbon and make a headband, sash, or cuff for your wrist. You can also incorporate old sequins or flat-back cabochons.

❖ INSTRUCTIONS ❖

Cut one yard of thread and thread through fine needle. Sew all buttons (except crystal buttons), beads, and crosses onto ribbon in random pattern, filling in most of surface. *Note:* Leave 1" on either end clear of beads.

Cut cord into three 1½" pieces. Fold each piece in half and sew ends together, creating ½" loops with ¼" tail.

Fold under ½" on each end of ribbon. Cover back side of ribbon using piece of ultra suede, or mole skin, stitching edges together to form lining. At one of end of ribbon, enclose tails of three cord loops between two layers, forming button loops. Sew three crystal buttons onto opposite end of bracelet for closure.

DESIGN TIP

SASH & HEADBAND PROJECTS

To create a beaded sash or headband you will need to start with a length of ribbon—44" for the sash and 18" for the headband.

Sew larger buttons onto ribbon and then fill in with smaller ones. *Note:* Keep in mind color and pattern, but also know that sometimes these ribbon sashes are truly stunning when they are encrusted in jewels. You can tie the sash in the back on an empire-waist dress or shirt, or wear it as a belt.

GLASS PEARL NECKLACES

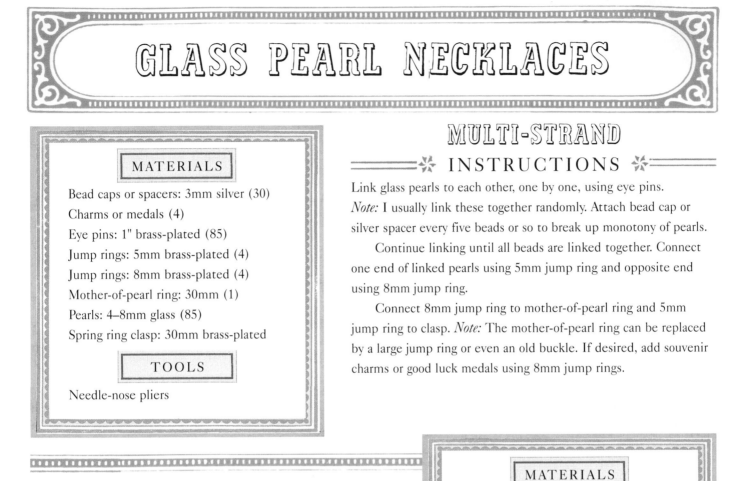

MATERIALS

Bead caps or spacers: 3mm silver (30)

Charms or medals (4)

Eye pins: 1" brass-plated (85)

Jump rings: 5mm brass-plated (4)

Jump rings: 8mm brass-plated (4)

Mother-of-pearl ring: 30mm (1)

Pearls: 4–8mm glass (85)

Spring ring clasp: 30mm brass-plated

TOOLS

Needle-nose pliers

MULTI-STRAND
❈ INSTRUCTIONS ❈

Link glass pearls to each other, one by one, using eye pins. *Note:* I usually link these together randomly. Attach bead cap or silver spacer every five beads or so to break up monotony of pearls.

Continue linking until all beads are linked together. Connect one end of linked pearls using 5mm jump ring and opposite end using 8mm jump ring.

Connect 8mm jump ring to mother-of-pearl ring and 5mm jump ring to clasp. *Note:* The mother-of-pearl ring can be replaced by a large jump ring or even an old buckle. If desired, add souvenir charms or good luck medals using 8mm jump rings.

PEARL RIBBON
❈ INSTRUCTIONS ❈

Thread each pearl onto an eye pin; cut and loop together using a bead-to-bead technique, which is also known as the rosary loop, by looping one bead to the next by cutting and looping the wire. At each end of strand, attach 5mm jump ring. Thread ribbon through jump rings. *Note:* The piece can be adjusted to fit as a necklace or a double-wrapped bracelet.

MATERIALS

Eye pins: 1" copper-ox (27)

Jump rings: 5mm copper-ox (2)

Pearl: 20mm ivory glass

Pearls: 7mm grey glass (5)

Pearls: 9mm silver glass (12)

Pearls: 11mm ivory glass (6)

Pearls: 15mm smoke glass (3)

Ribbon: ½"-wide grey striped silk (32")

TOOLS

Needle-nose pliers

... Amour et Psyché (détail) – (MUSÉE DU LOUVRE)   Don Zoubaloff

In Memoriam.

BEADED ROSARY

MATERIALS

Beads with large holes: 8mm crystal glass (78)

Cable chain: 4mm brass-plated (23")

Eye pins: 1" brass-plated (13)

Jump rings: 3mm (2)

Religious medal, cross, or charm

Seed beads 2mm crystal (24)

TOOLS

Flat-nose pliers

Needle-nose pliers

Wire cutters

I had never made a rosary before I designed this one. I pulled out an old child's rosary and copied the pattern. I chose very old beads with large holes as the prayer beads so that I could actually thread the small brass chain through the beads. I also found a brass charm with the image of Madonna in a mixed lot of charms I bought years ago. I chose to add more than the traditional number of beads so I could fit the piece over my head without a clasp.

═══ ❊ INSTRUCTIONS ❊ ═══

Cut chain into six 3½" pieces and two 1" pieces. Thread seed bead, glass bead, and seed bead onto eye pin and loop onto 3½" piece of chain. String ten glass beads onto chain.

Thread another seed bead, 8mm bead, and seed bead onto eye pin and link to end of first piece of chain. With opposite side of eye pin, attach another link of chain, and then thread ten more beads onto this link. Continue doing this up one side and down the opposite. *Note:* If you can't find medium-sized beads that can be threaded onto the small chain, you can link them together following the same pattern, just use additional eye pins.

To create drop: Attach 3mm jump ring to bottom of rosary. Thread another eye pin with seed bead, glass bead, and seed bead and loop onto chain. Loop opposite end of eye pin to piece of 1" chain and then attach three seed bead-glass bead-seed bead links. Attach remaining 1" piece of chain and one more bead combination. Finish by attaching charm or medal using 3mm jump ring.

Kaari Meng has been designing vintage glass jewelry for more than 20 years. Her first account, Bergdorf Goodman in New York City, ordered two dozen hatpins and soon after requested a complete line of beaded jewelry.

Kaari has exhibited at trade shows, designed for Anthropologie, and has sold her jewelry to specialty shops around the world. After experiencing all sides of jewelry manufacturing, she began teaching jewelry making out of her shop, French General, in Los Angeles, California.

Kaari and her husband, Jon, purveyors of French living, run a small business creating interesting merchandise such as laundry products, home décor accessories, and vintage beads and beading kits sold online at www.frenchgeneral.com and in stores throughout the United States, Europe, and Japan. French General also offers services including custom upholstery, interior consulting, and period decorating.

In 2005, Kaari was invited by Hallmark to be a keynote speaker on color and style trends. Her talk also covered the history and inspiration behind French General, followed by a visual montage of collections and creative ideas.

Kaari is the author of *The French-Inspired Home* (Lark/Chapelle, ©2006). Her home and shop have been featured in *Oprah, Martha Stewart Living, Mary Engelbreit's Home Companion, Country Living,* and *Romantic Homes* magazines.

Jon, Kaari, and daughter Sofia Zabala reside in California.

CREDITS

This book has been a long time in the making. Years ago, when I began collecting glass beads and baubles, I met people who understood their beauty and their rarity. So I collected, stashed, and hoarded beads for sixteen years.

Thank you to Jon Zabala for moving the beads many, many times. My whole family and many friends have worked for me at one point in their lives, so thank you to each and every one.

Molly, we had a great run in the jewelry business. Thanks for allowing me to string beads while you kept the show running.

I am constantly inspired by those who teach and I am lucky to have them close by. Ben Eagle, thank you for the one great dig and the one that got away. You are a teacher to me.

To Easy, who allowed me up to the balcony and beyond.

To Marcia, what a great old business this once was: Tinsel Trading Makes Great Trim.

To Jody Rice, who was sent to me by the jewelry bees.

To Eileen, Cathy, and Zac, thank you for your patience.

And now, finally, Sofia, this book is o-v-e-r.

METRIC EQUIVALENCY CHARTS

INCHES TO MILLIMETERS (MM) AND CENTIMETERS (CM)

Inches	mm	cm	Inches	cm	Inches	cm
⅛	3	0.3	9	22.9	30	76.2
¼	6	0.6	10	25.4	31	78.7
½	13	1.3	12	30.5	33	83.8
⅝	16	1.6	13	33.0	34	86.4
¾	19	1.9	14	35.6	35	88.9
⅞	22	2.2	15	38.1	36	91.4
1	25	2.5	16	40.6	37	94.0
1¼	32	3.2	17	43.2	38	96.5
1½	38	3.8	18	45.7	39	99.1
1¾	44	4.4	19	48.3	40	101.6
2	51	5.1	20	50.8	41	104.1
2½	64	6.4	21	53.3	42	106.7
3	76	7.6	22	55.9	43	109.2
3½	89	8.9	23	58.4	44	111.8
4	102	10.2	24	61.0	45	114.3
4½	114	11.4	25	63.5	46	116.8
5	127	12.7	26	66.0	47	119.4
6	152	15.2	27	68.6	48	121.9
7	178	17.8	28	71.1	49	124.5
8	203	20.3	29	73.7	50	127.0

YARDS TO METERS

yards	meters	yards	meters	yards	meters	yards	meters	yards	meters
⅛	0.11	2⅛	1.94	4⅛	3.77	6⅛	5.60	8⅛	7.43
¼	0.23	2¼	2.06	4¼	3.89	6¼	5.72	8¼	7.54
⅜	0.34	2⅜	2.17	4⅜	4.00	6⅜	5.83	8⅜	7.66
½	0.46	2½	2.29	4½	4.11	6½	5.94	8½	7.77
⅝	0.57	2⅝	2.40	4⅝	4.23	6⅝	6.06	8⅝	7.89
¾	0.69	2¾	2.51	4¾	4.34	6¾	6.17	8¾	8.00
⅞	0.80	2⅞	2.63	4⅞	4.46	6⅞	6.29	8⅞	8.12
1	0.91	3	2.74	5	4.57	7	6.40	9	8.23
1⅛	1.03	3⅛	2.86	5⅛	4.69	7⅛	6.52	9⅛	8.34
1¼	1.14	3¼	2.97	5¼	4.80	7¼	6.63	9¼	8.46
1⅜	1.26	3⅜	3.09	5⅜	4.91	7⅜	6.74	9⅜	8.57
1½	1.37	3½	3.20	5½	5.03	7½	6.86	9½	8.69
1⅝	1.49	3⅝	3.31	5⅝	5.14	7⅝	6.97	9⅝	8.80
1¾	1.60	3¾	3.43	5¾	5.26	7¾	7.09	9¾	8.92
1⅞	1.71	3⅞	3.54	5⅞	5.37	7⅞	7.20	9⅞	9.03
2	1.83	4	3.66	6	5.49	8	7.32	10	9.14

SUPPLIERS

Beadaholique
www.beadaholique.com
Craft beads, jewelry and beading
supplies

French General
www.frenchgeneral.com
Vintage beading, crafting supplies,
kits and tools

Splendor In The Glass
www.splendorintheglass.net
Vintage and antique glass beads,
stones and pendants

'Sweets' Beads
www.sweetsbeads.com
Costume jewelry supplies—everything
from plastic to semi-precious stones

Tinsel Trading
www.tinseltrading.com
Vintage millinery, trim and beads

York Beads
www.yorkbeads.com
Pressed glass, fire-polish, seed,
lampwork, semi-precious, wood,
and rhinestone beads

France

Victoria Broad
www.victoriabroad.com
Victoria Broad, 15 rue Hauteville,
75010 Paris

Venot, 147 rue du Temple,
75003 Paris

Fried Freres, 13 rue de Caire,
75002 Paris

La Droguerie, 9611 rue du Jour,
75001 Paris

INDEX

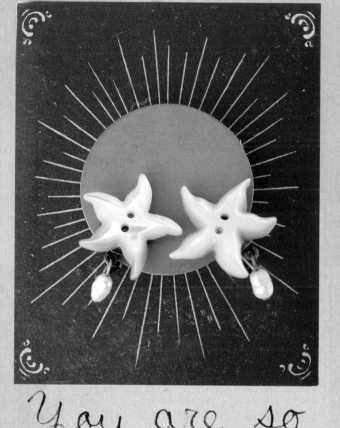

You are so
beautiful!